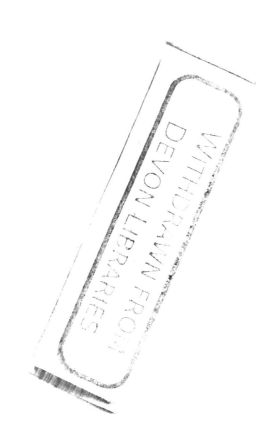

The
Diesel Shunter

The Diesel Shunter

Colin J. Marsden

OPC

An imprint of
Ian Allan Publishing

Half title: *In the days before warning ends were carried by locomotives and high-visibility clothing was mandatory, early-delivered standard 0-6-0 diesel-electric shunting locomotive No 13018 shunts at Crewe in mid-1954. CJM collection*

Title page: *This view at York has changed out of all recognition since it was taken on 6 July 1983. The massive works complex at York has virtually shut and most of the stabling and CCE sidings have been removed. Both the main line (to the left) and the York station avoiding lines in the foreground have been electrified, while track rationalisation has resulted in a totally changed view taken from the main road bridge at Skelton. Class 08 No 08501 painted in standard rail blue-livery shunts a short civil engineering train with a crane on the rear.* Colin J. Marsden

First published 2003

ISBN 0 86093 579 5

Published by Oxford Publishing Co

an imprint of
Ian Allan Publishing Ltd,
Hersham, Surrey KT12 4RG.
Printed by
Ian Allan Printing Ltd,
Hersham, Surrey KT12 4RG.

Code: 0310/A1

Contents

Introduction

Welcome to *The Diesel Shunter*. Perhaps of all the types or classes one could choose to write about, this sounds at first to be the most uninspiring. However, how wrong first thoughts can be, for over the last 20 years I have authored not one but two hardback books on the development of the UK diesel shunting locomotive.

When studied in depth, the subject of diesel shunting power is very interesting, far more in many respects than studying an individual class of main line traction. The story of diesel shunting traction dates back to the early 1930s, led by the then London Midland & Scottish Railway and quickly followed by the other 'Big Four' companies. On Nationalisation, the shunting story was far from settled, with much still to be sorted out in relation to design and deployment.

It is quite amazing that it was one of the mid-1930s LMS designs that, in much refined form, became the 'standard' large 0-6-0 diesel-electric shunting design under the BR 1950s orders, with a fleet size of well over 1,000 virtually identical locomotives being built by various BR workshops.

By virtue of their work remit, the 'standard' large shunter was not the answer to all needs of the rail industry and many small 0-4-0 designs were built, together with a greater number of non standard 0-6-0 locos. Many were constructed for specific duties, yards or areas, and sadly most of these had a very short life. The vast number of non-standard classes, which have certainly brought some interest to the pages of this book, were without exception deemed 'non-standard' under the BR National Traction Plan and withdrawn.

The BR 'standard' large 0-6-0 of Class 08 and 09 and the BR 'standard' small 0-6-0 of Class 03, have had a varied and interesting life. Standardisation was not the true word even at the time of the initial order, for different power units and generators were used, mainly to satisfy the requirement that not all eggs were placed in one basket! Over the years a mass of modifications were carried out to the 'standard' fleet; this started in BR days on a regional basis and became even more noticeable in privatisation.

One of the most obvious changes to the shunter fleets over the years has been livery. In the main, most fleets were delivered in BR black, changing from the late 1950s to BR green and then came the era of adding yellow/black wasp warning ends. BR rail blue came along from 1966; giving the longest period of a single livery until the numerous one-off, often silly, liveries were applied to shunting power in the immediate privatisation era.

Under privatisation the house colours of the owner/operator have been applied and by 2003 few BR rail blue locomotives were to be found.

In many cases the early withdrawal of BR shunter classes provided industrial operators with 'new' locomotives, often replacing steam. As the industrial rail users reduced, so along came the preservation movement which has found homes for literally dozens of shunting locomotives. A more recent twist to the shunter story has been a number of private operators, who have purchased spare shunting power from either the defunct BR or more recently the private operators, refurbishing their new charges and now hiring them back to main operators. Often these hire arrangements are more lucrative than passenger or small-size owners having the bother of owning perhaps one or just a handful of diesel locomotives.

I would like to record my thanks to the many photographers who have contributed to this title together with many retired employees of the private engineering companies who have shared their information about many of the prototype builds. The main UK rail industry and engineering companies have provided much useful information for this work and I express my thanks to them.

The technical tables at the start of each section have been, to say the least, challenging to compile. In many cases precise and accurate information has been almost impossible to find. In a number of cases information passed down over the years has now been proven to be incorrect. In a few instances, data is shown with the symbol '§' indicating that no definite confirmation of the item is available and, rather than perpetuate wrong information, the data has been omitted. If any readers can provide documentary evidence of any of the missing information, the author would like to receive this, so that if a reprint of this title is made, the data could then be added.

I do hope that readers will find this title as interesting to study as it was to compile and that the many modellers who have requested a reference work on *The Diesel Shunter* will enjoy browsing its pages.

Colin J. Marsden
Dawlish, Devon
September 2003

Diesel Shunter Development and the LMS Prototypes

In the main, the beginnings of diesel locomotive traction in the United Kingdom are usually reported as dating from the activities of the London Midland & Scottish Railway in the period 1931-33. However, it is worth recording that a quite amazing Priestman 12hp two-axle oil-engined shunting locomotive was built in 1884, using a wagon style underframe and a basic transversely mounted engine in the body of the 0-4-0 chassis. The 'locomotive' had a metal canopy roof, with a transverse wooden seat at one end. A large flywheel was located on one side and the driver sat between two box fuel tanks. The locomotive worked for a short time on the Alexandra Dock lines of the Hull & Barnsley Railway at Hull in 1894. At this time Diesel's first single-cylinder test engine was still undergoing initial trials.

Between 1898 and 1904 there were a few oil-engined locomotives of rather unusual external appearance built by Hornsby for the British War Office, these had engines of between 9 to 20hp which were the then 'modern' version of Akroyd Stuart's earlier work.

From these early beginnings, it was almost a quarter of a century before another oil-engined locomotive operated on UK railway lines, but it should be recorded that from around 1910 there had been a fair amount of building, particularly during the years of the Great War, of petrol-engined and petrol-paraffin powered locomotives of small size; these were the products of such firms as Hawthorn-Leslie, McEwan Pratt, Drewry, Kerr Stuart, Nasmyth Wilson, Motor Rail to name but a few.

By 1913 the Hawthorn-Leslie company was also quoting for oil-engined 'thermo' locomotives of up to 1,000hp. In the 1920s

Above: *How shunting was originally carried out, using a horse, 'coupled' to the draw-gear by a chain. This superb period piece was taken at Paddington.*
Author's collection

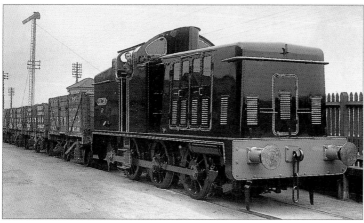

Left: *Built in 1936 at Vulcan Foundry, Newton-le-Willows and named* Vulcan, *this 0-6-0 mechanical transmission locomotive was fitted with a 275hp Vulcan-Frichs engine. It was of rounded design with a slightly off-centre cab. After working on loan with the LMS, the locomotive went into War Department use and after hostilities ended, it went to Yugoslavia for industrial use.*
Author's collection

Above: *Photographed during an advanced stage of conversion No LMS 1831 is seen on floor stands in Derby Works in June 1932. Although structurally assembled at Derby, the 400hp power unit came as an operational assembly from Davey-Paxman.* **Author's collection**

several builders became interested in the 'modern traction', but no oil-engined locomotives were sold for commercial use until 1928-29 when both Kerr Stuart and Avonside produced diesel-mechanical 'standard' locomotives designated shunting locomotives. These were followed in 1930 by Hudswell Clarke, who built a 'special' diesel locomotive of 330hp and this was followed in 1932 by Hunslet Engineering offering a 'standard' 150hp diesel shunter.

The first of the main line railways to become interested in new forms of traction, the London Midland & Scottish Railway (LMS) totally rebuilt a withdrawn Johnson Class 1F 0-6-0T steam locomotive No 1831 (Originally built as No 1361 at Vulcan Foundry in 1891) at its Derby Works into a then modern 'state-of-the-art' diesel 'tractor' unit, the original frames and wheels were retained, and a 400hp Paxman engine installed, together with a Haslam & Newton hydrostatic transmission system. A shoe-box type body was added to the chassis, which had a driving cab at each end with very small end windows. Vacuum train brakes were fitted. Authorised in October 1931, the locomotive emerged in November 1932 and cost the LMS just £5,967!

The locomotive's four-stroke 400hp Davey-Paxman power unit was positioned roughly in the place of the original boiler, the cooler radiators were roof mounted at the opposite end to equal out weight. The transmission consisted of a hydrostatic pump driven by crankshaft off the main power flange through

a universal coupling, the pump unit transferred power hydraulically to a transmission unit, located below, which gave a top speed of 25mph. Engine starting was effected by compressed air, to provide this a compressor was located in the equipment room, powered by a separate petrol engine. Braking on the locomotive was achieved by air, but a vacuum brake was provided for trains.

The locomotive gave little useful service, partly because of the lack of perseverance in regard to its transmission. Most of 1831s life was spent at Derby, but records show it was taken to London for demonstration to the directors of the LMS. No 1831 received various modifications and minor rebuilds in the years 1934-36. In late 1936 when a further round of upgrades were required, the LMS decided to terminate what they deemed as a trial with diesel traction and 1831 was stored. Its operational life was not however over, for after spending some four years in store, the locomotive was rebuilt again in 1940 into a mobile generator unit for provision of static power. Numbered MPU1831 and then MPU3, it worked in an un-powered form at Coventry and Crewe.

Though it seemed promising in some respects, faith in the 1831 project was low. However, when an internal LMS committee was formed to investigate means of single manning yard shunting locomotives, the committee quickly began looking at the trials with 1831 and made further investigation into diesel locomotive possibilities. At around this time, Hunslet Engine

Above: *In 1938 AEC at Southall built a 4-wheel diesel-mechanical; although owned by AEC, the locomotive operated some trials over the GWR Brentford branch. It was powered by a 78hp four-cylinder AEC engine, with a drive to both axles via a four speed gearbox. The locomotive had solid 'dish' wheels, and most remarkably the radiator was identical to that installed on AEC Regent III buses, then in production. The locomotive survived for many years as the AEC works pilot and is now preserved.*
Author's collection

Above: *This rather odd looking locomotive was an Armstrong-Whitworth/Sulzer demonstrator, it is seen on loan to the LMS at Preston Docks. It was fitted with a 250hp engine and had an electric transmission. This locomotive was deemed as the forerunner to LMS prototype No 7408 (7058).*
Author's collection

Right: *The same locomotive as in the picture above, is seen soon after delivery in 1932, when on loan to the LNER for evaluation of diesel shunting technology. On the left is a LNER K3 2-6-0. As can be seen, this early diesel prototype was fitted with train vacuum braking.*
Author's collection

Company emerged with a 150hp 21-ton MAN-engined powered shunter. Hunslet approached the LMS to allow testing of the design with an eventual view of selling the design to the railway.

With information available that production diesel shunting locomotives would soon be an alternative to steam traction, the LMS committee agreed to practical tests allowing builders and the LMS to gain some benefit. Thus was born the diesel shunter.

A total of seven prototype LMS diesel shunting locomotives were delivered in 1933-34, all fitted with a mechanical transmission, from four different builders and were fitted with no fewer than six different power units. We will look at these in numerical order.

7400 (7050): This 0-4-0 machine was supplied by the Drewry Car Co and erected at the Dick, Kerr Works of English Electric in Strand Road, Preston. It was built in mid-1934 and handed over to the LMS in November of the same year. Of the original

prototype fleet, this was the only four wheeled example, however it was much the same weight as its 0-6-0 sisters, just having a higher load per axle.

The power unit installed was an eight-cylinder four-stroke unit of 160hp supplied by W. H. Allen. It was fitted with an electric control system at 24V dc. Batteries were powered by a engine driven dynamo. The prime mover was designed by Allens to operate at a maximum of 182hp.

Engine water/oil cooling was provided by a nose mounted Serk radiator unit, belt driven from the main power unit. Transmission was mechanical and used a fluid coupling and epicyclic gearbox to a final drive unit on a jackshaft. Air for the locomotive was provided by two small compressors chain driven from a drive off the gearbox.

The outline of the locomotive had a tapered narrow-width bonnet section. The cab was much taller than the rest of the locomotive to provide operating staff a good all round view. The open sided cab was designed to allow a driver to operate

The Diesel Shunter

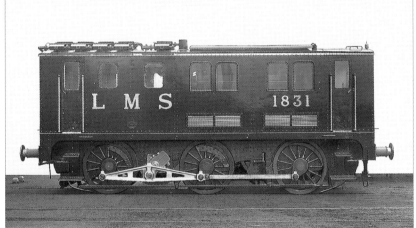

Above: *The first LMS diesel shunting loco, 0-6-0 diesel-hydraulic No 1831, this entered service from Derby Works in 1932. It was fitted with a Paxman engine and rebuilt from Midland Railway Class 1F No 1831. The design was just like a shoe box, with cab windows which were so small that forward vision must have been very difficult. A curiosity of this locomotive was a reversing mirror for the driver! No 1831 is seen at Derby on 20 July 1935 with Class 2P 4-4-0 No 459. This early attempt at LMS diesel traction was only moderately successful as it was stored in 1936 and later converted to a mobile power unit.*
Author's collection

Above: *In immaculate ex-shops condition, painted in black livery, with silver LMS decals and number, No 1831 poses for its official works picture. The locomotive's No 1 or principal driving end is on the left.*
Author's collection

Right: *After its short revenue earning life was over, No 1831 went into LMS Departmental stock as a mobile power unit and was used at both Derby and Crewe Works for power generation. With some quite significant bodywork modifications, No MPU1831 is seen at Crewe on 28 August 1949.*
Frank Hornby

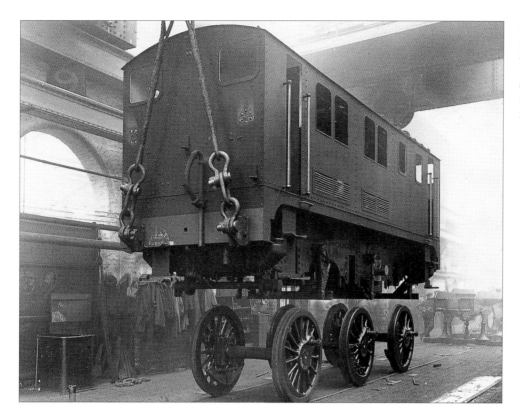

on either side of the cab and face either direction. The locomotive's top speed was 12mph.

The gear system was of the pre-selective type and changed gear at 3, 5, 8.5 and 12mph. Performance of this little locomotive was very impressive with shunting of trains of up to 400 tons being possible, and such was the power available that a take-up using 2nd gear was quite possible.

Following delivery, 7400, renumbered to 7050, was allocated to Agecroft, from where it was loaned to the War Department (Air Ministry) in August 1940. Its first operation took it to Stafford, but by October it was taken north to Leuchars in Scotland, where it remained until August 1941 when it was returned to the LMS. Under WD use the locomotive became No 25. On return to the LMS, the locomotive regained its number 7050 and was deployed again at Agecroft. In March 1943 it was sold to the War Department and was then recorded at a number of WD sites. Under the WD the locomotive had the numbers including 224, 70224, 846 and 240. Thankfully after its WD and later MoD use was over, No 7050 was preserved and is now at the Museum of Army Transport, Beverley, Yorkshire.

7401-7404 (7051-7054): The LMS gave Hunslet Engine Co of Leeds an order for four 0-6-0 locomotives with a common structural design, but each had different internal equipment.

The final example of the quartet also had a revised cab structure. Locomotive No 7401 (7051) was in fact the pioneer locomotive which started the prototype ordering back in 1932.

7401 (7051): This machine was fitted with a MAN 150hp 900rpm six-cylinder engine and had a separate two-cylinder petrol engine for starting the main power unit, this petrol engine was fired up from the cab and as the main engine took up speed, the petrol engine closed down. Transmission was by a multiple disc clutch and Hunslet gearbox connected via a Hardy-Spicer coupling. Four-speed gears were fitted giving a top speed of 30mph. Cooling of engine water and oil was by means of a nose radiator, belt driven from the main engine. A take-off from the power drive also drove the air compressor for locomotive air. The driving cab was designed for either side operation.

On delivery from Hunslet, the locomotive remained working in the Leeds area, but by 1936 it was working in Chester. In 1939 the locomotive was called into War Department use and went to the Ministry of Buildings and Works at Capenhurst near Chester, working as No 27. It returned to the LMS, again at Chester in mid-1941, only to return again for War use in August 1944. It returned to the LMS again in June of the following year and was withdrawn in December 1945 and returned to its builders in Leeds.

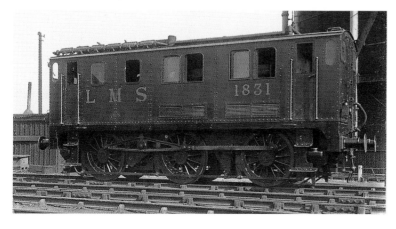

Left: *A side view of No 1831 soon after it entered service with the LMS.*
G. Ellis collection

The Diesel Shunter

Right & Below: *The very handsome tapered bonnet design of LMS No 7050 is shown from the left side. This 0-4-0 was built by the Drewry Car Co at the English Electric/ Dick, Kerr Works in Preston and at first operated within the confines of Preston Docks. It was later sold to the LMS and numbered 7050 (it was originally allocated the number 7400 which it never carried in service). These two pictures show the original clerestory roof to the cab, which was removed by the LMS in 1941. No 7050 was sold to the War Department in 1943 and is now preserved at the Museum of Army Transport at Beverley, Yorkshire.* **Both: Author's collection**

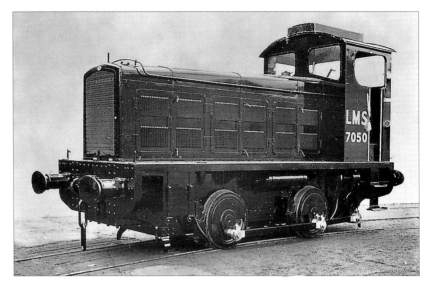

Below: *Hunslet Engine Co 1933-built No 7401, renumbered to 7051 was fitted with a MAN 6-cylinder 150hp power unit and drove a mechanical transmission. No 7051 was taken over by the Ministry of Works and Buildings at Capenhurst (Chester) in 1940 where it was renumbered 27 but was returned to the LMS in 1941. Between August 1944 and June 1945 it returned to War Department use and was sold back to its builders in December 1945.* **Author's collection**

Below & Below Right: *The sister locomotive to 7401 was 7402, which was eventually renumbered to 7052. The locomotive was built by Hunslet in 1934 and fitted with a McLaren-Benz 8M8D 150hp prime mover and a mechanical transmission. The illustration below, shows the locomotive in its original LMS condition as 7402, painted in grey workshop primer, while the view below right shows the machine renumbered to 7052 in LMS black livery, viewed from the opposite side. No 7052 was lent to the War Department at the Air Ministry from August 1940, returning to the LMS in 1942. It was eventually sold to the War Department (Ministry of Defence) and modified with flame proofing and was withdrawn in 1966 and scrapped in 1969.* **Both: Author's collection**

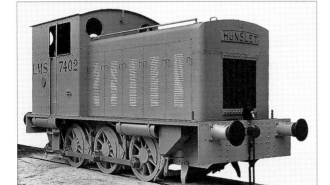

After being rebuilt and fitted with a McLaren diesel engine, the locomotive saw further use, not for the main stream railway but in industrial use. It first went to the London & Thames Haven Oil Wharves Ltd, working at Stanford-le-Hope between 1949-51, it later returned to Hunslet and was used as the works pilot. It was handed over to the Middleton Railway Trust in 1960. On the Middleton it was named *John Alcock*, after the man who kept Hunslet in railway business during the 1930s. The locomotive is still at the Middleton Railway today.

7402 (7052): The second of the Hunslet four, was powered by a McLaren-Benz 150hp unit operating at 1,000rpm which was an eight-cylinder engine. Starting was again by a separate two-cylinder petrol engine and was operated in the same way as 7401 above. Transmission was by a multiple-disc clutch and Hunslet gearbox connected via a Hardy-Spicer coupling. Two speed gears were fitted giving a top speed of just 8mph, restricting the locomotive to yard working. No 7402 onwards were slightly longer than the pioneer locomotive, measuring 24ft 8½in from buffer face to buffer face, compared to 23ft 2in on No 7401. Cooling was by the same means as No 7401.

After introduction, this locomotive remained working in the Leeds area until called-up for War department use in August 1940. The locomotive first went to the Air Ministry at Stafford, operating as No 24, it returned to the LMS in February 1942 at Leeds and was soon re-allocated to Nottingham. The locomotive was sold by Hunslet to the Admiralty in December 1943 and was substantially rebuilt and flame proofed for operations at the Royal Navy Armaments Depot, Broughton Moor near Maryport, here it worked as No 87. The locomotive remained in WD and then MoD use until 1966 when it was sold to Birds of Long Marston, at first it was used as a yard pilot, but after mechanical failure it was broken up in 1969.

7403 (7053): This example was fitted with a six-cylinder Brotherhood-Ricardo 150hp sleeve valve engine, set to operate at 1,200rpm. The engine was started by a compressed air motor, which engaged with a ring on the engine fly wheel, the air being supplied by a small compressor, which was 'charged' by a very small petrol-driven air generator. The locomotive's transmission was provided by David Brown, who developed a two-speed gearbox especially for the locomotive which could withstand the rigours of rail use. This transmission was a complex affair and the cause of many problems; it also incorporated the reversing mechanism. The structural design of the locomotive was the same as No 7402. The locomotive's top speed was 13¾mph.

After delivery and trials in Leeds No 7403 went to Plaistow in East London, it entered War Department service in October 1939 as No 23. It returned to the rail industry in January 1941 when it went to the Southern Railway as a pilot at Eastleigh Works, the following May it was again called up and went to the Admiralty. After a short period the locomotive was sold back to Hunslet at the end of 1942. Little is known of this locomotive after that time, until it was broken up by Hunslet Engineering of Leeds in 1954.

7404 (7054): The final locomotive of this 'fleet' was the most powerful, being fitted with a six-cylinder 180hp Paxman engine which operated at 900rpm. Engine starting was very similar to 7403. The transmission was again different, after the fluid coupling a free wheel, a drive shaft and a rocking brake were located, which held the shaft during gear changing. A Hunslet design three-speed gearbox was installed. The locomotive's top speed was 13mph. The structural design of this locomotive was slightly different from the others, the most noticeable change was the provision of windows in both front and back 'walls'.

On delivery 7404, which was actually numbered 7054, worked at Leeds before being transferred to Derby. The locomotive was called to War Department use in June 1940,

Below: *Another of the early Hunslet products was 7404, later renumbered to 7054. This locomotive was built in 1934 and fitted with a 180hp Davey Paxman 6V25 engine driving a mechanical transmission. No 7054 remained in LMS use during World War II. It was withdrawn in 1954 and sold to the National Coal Board. In 1960 it was rebuilt with a Rolls Royce C6N engine and remained in service until 1974.*
Author's collection

The Diesel Shunter

but remained with the LMS until November when it went to Longmoor in Hampshire as No 26, being used for instructional duties. It was returned to the LMS in July 1941, operating from Speke Junction, Liverpool. In May 1943 the locomotive was officially withdrawn and handed to the War Department, this time as No 225, working originally at Highbridge and then Bicester before being re-sold back to Hunslet.

The locomotive after a major refit in Leeds, was hired to the National Coal Board in 1954 and was later sold to this Government body. The NCB funded a further major refit in 1960 when a Rolls Royce C6N engine was installed before it started working at Brodsworth Colliery, Doncaster. The locomotive was retired from the NCB in 1974 and broken up at NCB Hickleton Main.

7405-7406 (7055-7056): This pair of machines were very reminiscent of 0-6-0 steam locomotives, even down to a chimney at the non-driving end! Built on a 26ft 10^1/$_2$in frame, the two were built by Hudswell Clarke & Co Ltd and were fitted with a Mirrlees-Ricardo 150hp prime mover. This was started by direct air supplied by a compressor powered by a small petrol engine. The transmission was a fluid coupling from the engine to a three speed gearbox which contained the reversing mechanism, a carden shaft drive was fitted to a worm gear on one axle. A large radiator was fitted at the nose end, which was chain driven off an engine flange, as were two air compressors for locomotive supply.

After construction the two locomotives operated for several months around Leeds before the LMS officially took them into stock, working from Speke, Liverpool. Their operating career was however very short and in mid-1939 both were withdrawn. With the outbreak of world hostilities, the pair were not immediately broken up and in 1940 both were converted to mobile power units (MPUs) and renumbered MPU2 and MPU1. Both were initially used at Coventry, before moving to Crewe. MPU1 remained on the LMS/LM, working at Crewe and Kilmarnock, while MPU2 went into Eastern

Above: Another view of LMS No 7054, showing the 'B' side of the loco, Compared to Nos 7051-7053, this was a far more substantial locomotive, with a much larger driving cab, having full width cab windows both front and back. No train braking was provided.
Author's collection

Region stock under BR and went to Doncaster, Stratford and eventually Thornaby; on the ER it became No 953 Mobile Diesel Set.

7407 (7057): This 0-6-0 locomotive is of quite significant interest as it was built by Harland & Wolff of Belfast, Northern Ireland and shipped to England for use by the LMS, and is to date the only Irish-built locomotive to have been used on a main line railway in Britain.

The locomotive was built in 1934 and was of general 0-6-0 steam locomotive appearance. After construction, during a

Below: Hudswell Clarke's input to the 1930s locomotive trials was with two, almost steam-outline machines Nos 7055 and 7056. Both were fitted with Mirrlees-Ricardo 150hp engines. No 7056 is shown from its A side painted in LMS black livery.
Author's collection

Above: *In terms of their main line railway career, the two Hudswell Clarke machines had a very short operating life. The pair were used for many months after construction in the Leeds area, before being taken officially into LMS stock in 1934 at Speke, Liverpool. By mid-1939 the pair were withdrawn from the capital fleet and modified as mobile (in terms of having wheels) power units, numbered MPU2 and MPU1. MPU2 was later rebuilt by Stratford and emerged as Mobile Diesel Set 953, (see page 237).*
Author's collection

period of testing, problems were identified and the locomotive was delayed in entering service with the LMS until the end of 1936. The locomotive's prime mover was a Harland & Wolff built two-stroke unit, known as 'Harlandic'. It had a number of unusual features having airless injection and a scavenger blower, gear driven off the engine crankshaft. One serious problem with the locomotive was noise, with special silencers installed before entry into service. Starting of the locomotive required the pre-heating of 'glow-plugs' to warm the cylinder, this being achieved by using battery power.

The transmission consisted of a hydraulic coupling on the engine connected to a two speed gearbox, incorporating a reversing mechanism, this was connected to the wheelsets by a worm drive on the leading axle. The radiator at the nose end was shaft driven from the engine, air for locomotive braking was provided by an engine driven compressor.

On delivery to Britain, the locomotive was allocated the identity 7057 and allocated to Chester, it later worked at Heysham for a short period until it was sold back to Harland & Wolff in January 1945, after being taken out of service 12 months before. Back in Ireland it was overhauled, converted to 5ft 3in gauge and used by the Northern Counties Committee (NCC). During its rebuild, the engine was exchanged for a more powerful 225hp example and the equipment compartment was extended to full cab height. It was then numbered 22. The locomotive was subsequently transferred to the Ulster Transport Authority, the successor to the NCC and remained in service until April 1965.

The First Diesel-Electrics
In 1934 the LMS purchased from Armstrong-Whitworth a 250hp 40-ton single-motor diesel-electric shunting locomotive, and later the same year gave facilities to English Electric for the service trial of that builder's initial three-axle two-motor diesel-electric shunter, a 300hp output and 47 tons unit. Compared with the then standard 0-6-0T of 49 tons weight, the work of these two diesel-electrics was quite outstanding, in regard to loads started and hauled, effective work in a shift period, and an ability to maintain 24 hour a day service for up to seven days. Soon the LMS traffic department pressed strongly for more of the diesel-electric builds, but in a rather larger size for use in the bigger yards and on the heaviest shunting duties.

Thereafter the original plan of the LMS to introduce small diesel-mechanical or hydraulic units was more or less forgotten, at least until after railway Nationalisation in 1948, with the policy turning towards building diesel-electric machines, suited mainly to the larger yards and heaviest hump shunting work as well as the ability to perform main line trip working. No more 150/200bhp locomotives were built until after the formation of British Railways, except for a Drewry shunter on the LNER in the mid-1940s, and for one or two departmental locomotives of smaller power output.

Although it was the original desire of the traffic department to operate yard and shunting power with just one man in the cab, this was largely put on the back burner in favour of quickly getting a number of powerful machines into traffic to ease the general problems in yards. This received support from C. E. Fairburn who had recently joined the LMSR as deputy chief mechanical and electrical engineer, from English Electric, and a man who strongly influenced the switch in trend to diesel-electric traction.

The Vital Step

In 1935 an order was placed for 20 diesel-electric shunters, which were delivered in 1936. Ten were from Armstrong Whitworth, and were developed from the 250hp machine. They had an Armstrong-Sulzer 350/400hp 875rpm engine and a single spring-borne Crompton Parkinson traction motor driving the wheels through double reduction spur gears, jackshaft and side rods. The 10 units from The English Electric Company were developed from their prototype 300hp unit. These had an English Electric 350hp 680rpm engine, and two nose-suspended traction motors one on each outer axle, all wheels being coupled by side rods. Both design types had a top speed of 22mph, and initiated the UK railway practice of having a low top speed for greater shunting power. The Armstrong Whitworth

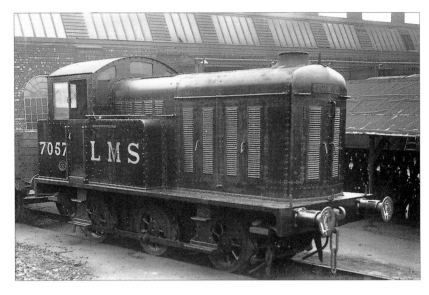

Right & Below: *This locomotive was a real rarity in the prototype shunters. It was built by Harland & Wolff in Belfast and is thus the only locomotive built in Ireland for use in Britain. After construction the locomotive was found to be a little problematic and was shipped to Britain in 1935, taking up service the following year. The view right shows the locomotive in LMS black livery while working from Chester. The illustration below shows the locomotive in as delivered works primer. Note the superb Harlandic name on the radiator end, this was the trading name formed by Harland & Wolff for their railway assembly division.*
Both: Author's collection

The Diesel Shunter

locomotives weighed 50 tons with 635 gallons of fuel, and the English Electric units weighed in at 51 tons with 500 gallons of fuel. Thus another long-standing feature of UK practice commenced, that of a large fuel tank with capacity for up to a week or more of work with up to 24 hours-a-day operation. The results given from early trials by these locomotives confirmed the expectations from the two prototypes, with both types returning a 'very satisfactory' performance, the English Electric fleet had a wheelbase of 11 ft 6 in and this was easier on curves than the 14 ft 6 in wheelbase of the Armstrong Whitworth locos, but on the other hand the steam locomotives they replaced mostly had a wheelbase of 16 ft 6 in.

In 1937 the Armstrong Whitworth company surprisingly left the locomotive construction business, and it could then be expected that the way was clear for future orders to be placed for the English Electric two-traction-motor design. However

Below: Between May 1935 and November 1936, 10 locomotives, Nos LMS 7059 - LMS 7068 emerged from Armstrong Whitworth, conforming to the basic 'standard' shunter design. These jackshaft 0-6-0 diesel-electric units had a Sulzer power unit. No 7059 in ex-works condition is seen at the Armstrong Whitworth factory.
Author's collection

The Diesel Shunter

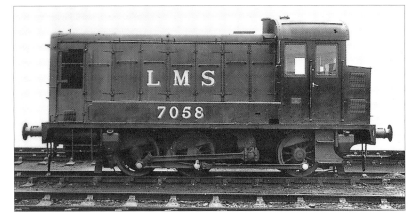

Right: This broadside view of No 7058 clearly shows the different wheel spacing of this Armstrong Whitworth design. The wheelbase between the leading wheelsets was 4ft 6in, while the wheelbase between the middle and rear wheel sets was 8ft, thus allowing for the jackshaft assembly. No 7068 is seen in black LMS livery.
Author's collection

the feeling for a single spring-borne motor and jackshaft drive arrangement was so strong in the mechanical and motive power departments following experience of 20 locomotives in 1936, that when another 40 machines were ordered they were given the English Electric 350 bhp engine, but powering a single spring-borne traction motor with double reduction gears and jackshaft drive, fitted with English Electric control gear. This batch was important in another direction as it introduced the practice of UK railways' building on a large scale the mechanical portions of diesel locomotives in their own works, and only buying-in power, transmission and control equipments. The previous 20 locomotives for the LMS had been obtained complete from the private builders.

The actual introduction, on a small scale, of the railway building its own mechanical portions for diesels came in 1937,

when, in its endeavours to sell its proven diesel-electric shunter to the other three railway companies (Great Western Railway, Southern Railway and London & North Eastern Railway), The English Electric Co agreed with the SR that the latter would build a batch of three mechanical portions (SR1-3) at Ashford, and send them north to the EE works in Preston for English Electric power, transmission and control equipments to be installed. The fully-functional locomotives were then sent south again to the SR. In a curiosity which only seems to occur in railway circles, these three SR 'standard' locomotives were 1ft 9 in longer than the LMS 'standard' design and weighed 55 tons against 51 tons of the earlier build; however the trio had the same 30,000 lb tractive effort. The GWR entered the main stream diesel shunter programme in 1936 when it acquired one 'standard' locomotive of the English Electric design, but this was supplied complete by EE.

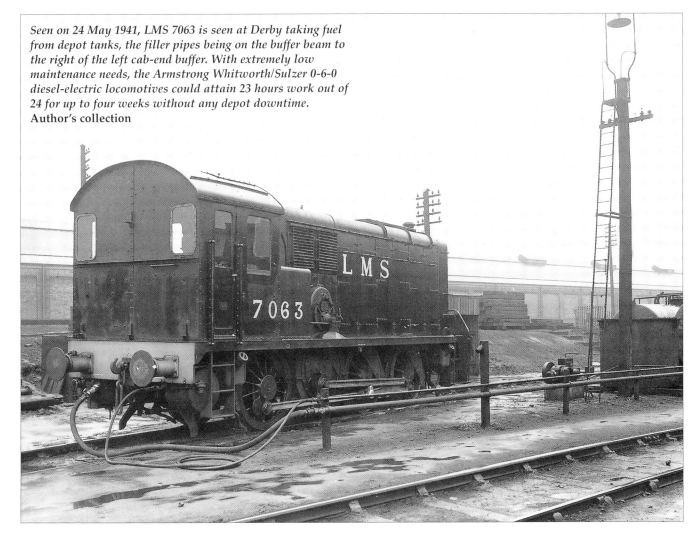

Seen on 24 May 1941, LMS 7063 is seen at Derby taking fuel from depot tanks, the filler pipes being on the buffer beam to the right of the left cab-end buffer. With extremely low maintenance needs, the Armstrong Whitworth/Sulzer 0-6-0 diesel-electric locomotives could attain 23 hours work out of 24 for up to four weeks without any depot downtime.
Author's collection

Wartime Developments

The 40 LMS locomotives mentioned above began to appear in 1939, but delivery was not finished until 1941. In the meantime, 10 were built at the LMS Derby works in 1940, and were drafted direct to the War Department, and only 30 locomotives (which became Nos 12003-12032) were actually put into operation by the LMS. During the war years 1939-1945, 18 of the LMS diesel-electric shunting locos, including all 10 of the Armstrong Whitworth locomotives of 1936, were transferred into War Department service.

Early in the war, one of the 1936 batch of English Electric shunters was rebuilt with two force ventilated nose-suspended traction motors and double-reduction gears in order to make it more suitable for the normal duties of hump

shunting. This modification was subsequently applied to the next batch of diesel-electric locomotives ordered — six English Electric type locomotives, LMS Nos 7120-7125, built in 1945, and which in a sense set the pattern for the later post 1948 British Railways standard diesel-electric shunter, although of course this line *can* be traced back to the prototype of 1934. This order for six locomotives was the first of a much larger order, because as the war ended in 1945, the LMS drew up a construction programme for 100 new 0-6-0 diesel-electric shunting locomotives to be completed by the end of 1952. These became Nos 12033-12138; all were built at Derby Works and were fitted with English Electric 6K engines, two 135hp nose-suspended double-reduction traction motors supplied as traction packages by English Electric in Preston for installation at the point of mechanical construction.

In 1944-5 the LNER entered the diesel shunting locomotive market, building at its Doncaster 'Plant' factory four modified 'standard' 0-6-0 machines with English Electric 6K power units and double-reduction gear motors. The order for these locomotives was rather unusual as it specified that connections be made to enable the locomotives to be used as mobile power plants as well as for shunting traction. These locomotives weighed in at 50 tons, and were numbered 15000-15003. In 1947 Doncaster works built the frames for and Brush completed a fifth locomotive, No 15004, which was powered by a Petter 360hp two-stroke engine as a trial.

This page: No 12010, illustrated above and below, was one of a batch of 20 locomotives built in 1939, which cost at the time just £6,100 each. The original LMS 7087 became BR No 12010 and allocated to Willesden depot in North London for many years until replaced by 'standard' units. No 12010 was then moved north to Crewe. These two illustrations show the locomotive at Willesden and Toton. The illustration below shows BR black livery complete with the Lion over Wheel logo. Author's collection/E. Blakey

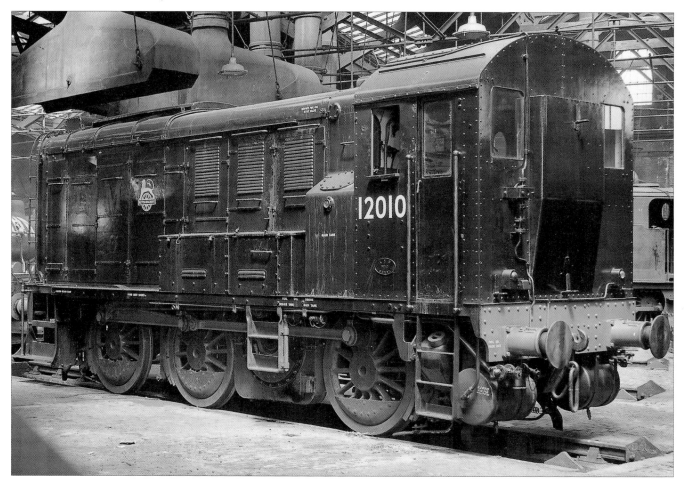

Above: *Carrying number M7117 with early British Railways branding, this view shows the locomotive shunting at Willesden just after Nationalisation. M7117 was later renumbered 12030.*
H. C. Casserley

Right: *In black livery with BR Lion over Wheel logo on the engine room side, No 12022 is seen at Crewe in 1961.*
C. M. Kempson

Below: *Painted in LMS black-livery with a red buffer beam, No 7081 is viewed on the hump at Toton just prior to Nationalisation. This view clearly shows the cab end layout with the protruding centre section of the cab.*
Author's collection

Left: *Some of the original jackshaft locos, such as No 12020 survived long enough to be repainted in standard BR green with full yellow/black wasp ends. No 12020 is seen at Newton Heath, Manchester in May 1960.*
J. E. Wilkinson

Right: *All of the LMS batch 7059-7068 went into War Department service at various times. LMS No 7063 is seen here as WD883 at MoD Bicester in 1961. This locomotive was one of two which remained in the UK and did not see overseas service.*
A. Swain

Below: *WD70051 (ex LMS 7102) is seen on the Port Said to Suez main line at Faycd in Egypt on 21 April 1952. The locomotive is hauling a short supplies train. This locomotive was later taken into the stock of the Egyptian State Railway as No 4016.*
G. F. Bannister

The Diesel Shunter

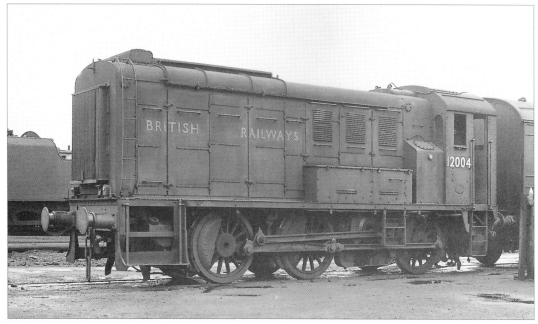

Right: *With the full name British Railways on the engine room side, No 12004, the original No 7081, is seen at Willesden on 12 July 1953.*
Derek Porter collection

Above: *LMS No 7072 is seen under construction at the English Electric Works in Preston in 1935. The English Electric six-cylinder 'K' series engine is seen being lowered into position with its English Electric generator already attached. Unlike some of the other locomotives built at this period the main bodywork had previously been assembled and the power unit assembly dropped into position through the roof opening. LMS7072 only worked with the LMS until April 1940 when it was sent by the War Department to France, where it was officially written off the following December.*
Author's collection

Below & Right: *On the right we see the official LMS view of 1935-built No 7070, while below we see the English Electric model of the same loco, as presented to the LMS at the time of the order being placed. LMS No 7070 was the second of what can be described as the original series of 'standard' 0-6-0 diesel-electric locomotives and many of the features of this build were incorporated in subsequent LMS builds and indeed the 1950s BR 'standard' shunting locomotive orders.* Both: Author's collection

Below: *LMS No 7079 was built as an English Electric demonstrator and taken into LMS capital stock in 1936. This locomotive had a number of detail differences from the production batch to which it was numerically attached. Originally it was rated at 300hp and was so significantly 'non-standard' that the LMS required that English Electric change its specification before purchase. These changes documented as costing £5,000 would not be carried out by EE, instead the builders supplied the standardisation parts to the railway, with the upgrade work being done at Crewe Works. This work included upgrading the engine to 350hp and the retention of the original vacuum brakes, which were usually isolated. Obviously differences were still present, as its weight was recorded by the LMS as four tons lighter than the production batch. No 7079 is seen in LMS black livery at Crewe on 16 August 1936. It was later taken into BR stock as No 12002.* R. C. Riley

The Diesel Shunter

Left: *Compared with the above illustration, No 7070 when seen at Crewe South shed on 16 August 1936 was looking rather tatty, with a fuel spill down the side of the fuel tank, and the body looking rather grubby.*
R. C. Riley

Below: *Of the 7069-7078 'production' series of 0-6-0s, only this locomotive, No 7074, remained with the LMS throughout the war, all others operated for the War Department. This locomotive was modified in 1940 with double reduction gears and forced ventilation of the traction motors to assist in hump shunting.*
Author's collection

Above & Right: *In terms of photographic line-ups, these two views taken at Crewe for the official LMS photographer have to rate as some of the finest. The pictures were taken at Crewe South on 17 August 1936 to demonstrate the delivery of the batch of ten 'standard' 0-6-0 diesel-electric units.*
Both: Author's collection

Three locomotives of the LMS 7069-7079 series survived into BR numbering, with Nos 7074, 7076 and 7078 becoming 12000-12002. No 12000 is seen here at Derby on 1 April 1958.
P. H. Groom

The Diesel Shunter

Post-war position

By 1946, it was not untrue to say, the LMS, with around 40 diesel-electrics in service, was further advanced in diesel shunting locomotive practice than *any* other railway in the world — outside of the USA. There was very exact knowledge of what the locomotives could do in terms of shunting and yard work, and new introductions were being made in fresh areas with little or no teething troubles. The specifications for each batch built from 1936 onwards were carefully drawn up, and were wholly progressive, and devoted to obtaining without doubt 24 hour a day performance for a minimum of a week and by the late 1940s for a lot longer.

A careful maintenance schedule was also devised and the staff educated and encouraged to keep to work and to develop ways of improvement. To improve reliability, in a 1937 specification came the introduction of a hump yard shunting duty cycle of 25 minutes, which could be maintained *continuously* with a time gap of just 5 minutes between each cycle to 'cool off'. After the end of hostilities, by 1947, a major maintenance programme for the diesel fleet had been devised. Then mainly of the single, spring-borne motor type, it was based on maintenance, inspection and work every 12/16 days, 24/32 days, 160/190 days, and 320/380 days, and involved an intermediate overhaul only at 26,000 to 30,000 miles and a heavy overhaul at between 52,000 and 60,000 miles. As the actual speed of UK shunting locomotives was just 5mph, but in reality the actual speed in the yards over 24-hour period averaged at $1^{1}/_{2}$-2mph, these staggering miles would have taken a long time to achieve. In subsequent post BR days the overhaul programme became based on time rather than miles, with around 30,000 to 35,000 hours in traffic running between heavy overhauls the norm.

Between the end of the war in 1945 and the beginning of British Railways on 1 January 1948, the four main group railways (LMS, GWR, SR and LNER) put in hand further orders for standard 350hp diesel shunting locos, though many of these were not delivered until after Nationalisation. The LMS and LNER activities are mentioned above. Swindon Works of the GWR put in hand construction of six of the English Electric standard locomotives of 50 tons weight; while SR's Ashford works built 26 locomotives of the Ashford/EE type, but were again non-standard at only 45 tons, or 10 tons less than the original Ashford-built locomotives, and had a maximum tractive effort of 24,000lb. against the standard 30,000lb.

Deliveries of these locomotives took a few years after Nationalisation. Meanwhile, British Railways, under the Railway Executive, had drawn up a new 'standard' design for diesel shunting power, based closely on the LMSR/EE type, but with various modifications to suit a wide diversity of line conditions, yards and loading gauges. It was also announced, that although the 'standard' locomotive was to be based on the well tried English Electric 6K engine and EE generator unit, the locomotive frames, body casing and other parts were to be 'suitable' for the installation of power unit/generator groups from other manufacturers offering a similar power, weight, speed and bulk, this resulted from massive pressure placed on the rail industry from other oil-engine building companies who could see a monopoly in power unit supply by EE. The BR made no attempt prior to its 1950s shunter modernisation plan orders to get an up-to-date shunting locomotive design, based not only on experience gained since the late 1930s, but

Below: *Painted in BR black livery, No 12009 is seen at Willesden on 11 October 1953. The 'shunter' is standing on a special step area, found on many of the prototype and production shunters, providing ground staff with a relatively safe place to stand, without having to return to the driving cab.*
A. R. Carpenter

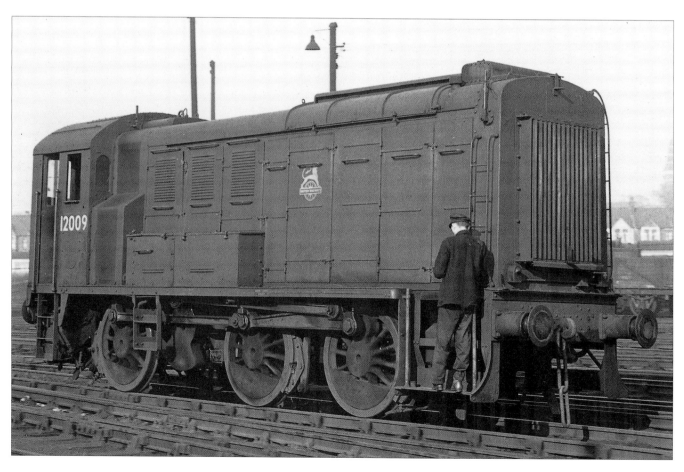

The Diesel Shunter

also on the equipment and knowledge then available to the industry and thus the design remained and indeed still does today, essentially what it was in the batch of 10 locomotives built in 1936, one major modification being the force-ventilated double-reduction traction motors.

The standard length of 29ft 3in over buffers and an 11ft 6in wheelbase were retained, but to get improved rail clearance the wheel diameter was increased from 48 inches to 54 inches, a diameter which had previously been used by all the locomotives built by the Southern Railway; it is interesting to note that the single-motor LMS locos, Nos 12003-32 weighing 54 tons had 51 inch wheels.

The output of the English Electric 6KT engine was increased by 50hp to 400hp working at the same speed of 680-685 rpm, an increase which the engine was able to take without structural changes. The locomotive weight with English Electric equipment, and with fuel, oil and water tanks full, was standardised at 49 tons, giving a maximum axle load of 16.33 tons, and a starting tractive effort of 35,000lb, equal to 32 per cent adhesion. Top track speed was 20mph, and the Wiseman double-reduction gears of the two traction motors had a ratio of 23.9 to 1. The air-brake compressor was motor-driven, and two vacuum exhausters for train brakes were provided.

Under the major re-equipment plan, a first order for 25 equipments for the new 'standard' shunter model was placed with English Electric, with an order for mechanical parts awarded not surprisingly to the former LMS works in Derby; these units were delivered in 1953. In the summer of that year a further order for 45 sets of power and transmission control equipment was placed with English Electric, along with an order for 15 sets of equipment comprising Blackstone 350hp engines and British Thomson-Houston electrical equipment, another 15 equipments were made up of Blackstone 350hp engines and General Electric Company (GEC) electrical equipment, a third order for 10 sets of Crossley two-stroke engines and Crompton Parkinson electrical equipment was made, thus satisfying the desire of other engine and equipment manufacturers to have a hand in the shunter project. After this no further trials of other power units or electrical equipment were used with standardisation of the EE equipments.

Diesel-Mechanical Types

After a gap of some 18 years with one lone break, on the LNER after 13 years, the original remit of the LMS 1931 committee was once again taken up, when it was realised there were many locations where the 350hp locomotives was just too big to operate and that there existed a considerable need for the deployment of a basic 200hp 30ton machine, a fact fully realised by the LMS committee, but rejected by Fairburn.

In 1952 the Drewry Car Company supplied a batch of 10 of its standard 204hp three-axle locomotives with Gardner 8L3 engines, Fluidrive coupling, and Wilson four-speed gearbox, four of this fleet were fitted with 'skirts' as *tram* locomotives for service at Yarmouth and on the Wisbech-Upwell line. These locomotives weighed 27 tons. Several subsequent orders were placed for Drewry 204hp locomotives and that maker also received substantial orders for power, transmission and control equipments for installation in mechanical structures built in works of British Railways. Actually Drewry's first order for this type of shunter was placed by the LNER just prior to nationalisation.

Meanwhile, beginning in 1952 Barclay, Hunslet and Hudswell Clarke all began to receive orders for 204 bhp diesel-mechanical locomotives with the same Gardner power unit but with different transmission systems except for the Barclay units in which the fluid coupling and Wilson box were retained. In 1955 some even smaller two-axle locomotives for special locations such as Ipswich docks were ordered from Hunslet, Barclay and Ruston & Hornsby. With this need having been met, a return was made to the three-axle 204hp type and substantial orders were placed over the next few years with the private makers and BR workshops. The rest of the shunter story can be found in the following sections.

SR Ashford 0-6-0 diesel-electric SR1-3 15201-15203

The Southern Railway, which always liked to be slightly different, ordered three 'standard' diesel-electric locomotives in 1936 for delivery in 1937. These were ordered by R. E. L. Maunsell, the SR CME for comparative tests against his Class Z 0-8-0 steam locos. The term 'standard' could be applied as the traction package was the quickly becoming standard English Electric 6K, powering an EE alternator group and feeding two English Electric traction motors.

The mechanical portion was assembled by the Southern Railway at its Ashford shops in Kent and in principle followed the previous LMS designs, except that it was slightly heavier (4 tons) and had larger diameter driving wheels — 4ft 6in compared to 4ft 0$\frac{1}{2}$in of the LMS design. These larger diameter wheels were stipulated as the locomotives were destined to operate over third rail electrified areas, and the extra wheel diameter gave the necessary clearance.

These were the first British diesel-electric shunters built at a railway owned workshop as opposed to a private industrial site.

The top speed of the Southern trio was 30mph, this increase over the LMS design was stipulated as the fleet was proposed to operate main line 'trip' workings between stations, yards or sidings, this relatively low speed made it possible to fit such workings in with the growing Southern Railway passenger schedule.

When the three locomotives emerged between July-September 1937, all were painted in all over black livery, carrying the legend Southern on the side fuel tank, with the locomotive running number 1, 2 or 3 below. Originally the fleet were shown as numbers 958-960, but this was altered to a new series for diesel traction while under assembly. The locomotives use by the

Southern Railway was short lived, as from 1941 until 1945 all three were conscripted into Government War Department service, working at various sites.

After their return to the Southern the trio operated from Norwood Junction until being taken into BR ownership from nationalisation in January 1948. Under BR ownership, the locomotives became Nos 15201-15203 in the standard BR diesel numeric range.

The original black livery eventually gave way to BR green, with numbers and BR lion and wheel logo applied to the cab side. The Southern Region of BR later applied the five digit numbers on the red buffer beams in white.

When ordered, no train brakes were stipulated, speed retardation being achieved by a direct air brake on the locomotive. Front and rear marker lights were not carried as a fixture on the loco, with oil powered marker and tail lights being 'hung-on' as required. Lamp irons were provided on both ends onto which SR-style white marker discs were hung.

An unusual design feature of this fleet was the slight overhang of the cab upper section over the buffers, in which two windows were provided, giving the cab staff good visibility of the coupling. This was especially useful for 'buffing-up' and a feature many locomotive men would have liked to have seen carried forward into the standard BR 0-6-0 diesel-electric shunter range.

The fleet of three SR prototype but 'standard' 0-6-0 shunting locomotives remained in traffic allocated to Eastleigh, Ashford and Norwood until late 1964 when all three were withdrawn. Sadly none were preserved and all three were broken up in South Wales.

Left: *Southern No 3, painted in black livery and viewed from its cab end, is seen 'on shed' and obviously under repair at Norwood Junction on 28 April 1948. The hinged roof section is seen to be open, providing access to the top of the English electric power unit, while two of the removable body side doors are open allowing inspection and repair of the engine and other equipment.*
N. F. Parker

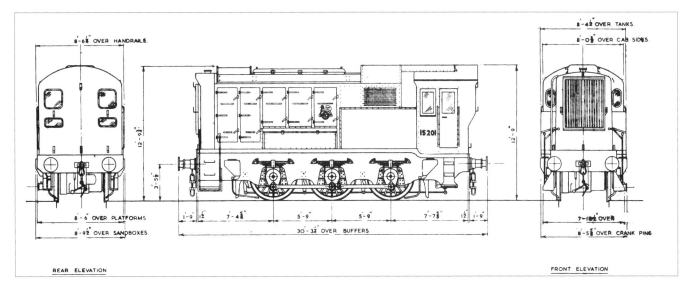

REAR ELEVATION   FRONT ELEVATION

Southern Railway number range:	SR1-SR3	Cylinder bore:	10in
BR 1948 number range:	15201-15203	Cylinder stroke:	12in
Former class codes:	D3/12, later 3/9A	Maximum speed:	30mph
Built by:	SR Ashford	Brake type:	Air on loco, no train brakes
Year introduced:	1937	Brake force:	24 tons
Wheel arrangement:	0-6-0	Route availability:	Not issued
Weight:	55 1/2 tons	Heating type:	Not fitted
Height:	12ft 9in	Multiple coupling type:	Not fitted
Length:	30ft 3 1/4in	Main generator type:	EE801
Width	8ft 5 5/8in	Aux generator type:	EE736
Wheelbase:	11ft 6in	Traction motor type:	DK129-2D
Wheel diameter:	4ft 6in	No of traction motors:	2
Min curve negotiable:	3 chains	Gear ratio:	§
Engine type:	English Electric 6KT	Fuel tank capacity:	490gal
Engine output:	350hp	Lub oil capacity:	120gal
Power at rail:	194hp	Sanding equipment:	Pneumatic
Tractive effort:	30,000lb		

Southern No 1, in as delivered black livery with a yellow 'Southern' legend and No 1 on the frame mounted fuel tank. This picture was taken just days after delivery to Norwood in the autumn of 1937, before the machine entered normal service. **Author's collection**

Above: *The cab layout design of the three SR prototype shunters, with the slightly over-hanging upper section with angled windows, allowing views of the buffer beam during shunting operations was a considerable improvement on steam traction. SR No 1 is seen shunting at Norwood yard in 1945.*
Author's collection

Left: *Southern No 2 was conscripted to War Department service between 1941 and 1945 and was used at Martin Mill Military Railway near Dover. The locomotive is seen after return to the Southern at Norwood Junction on 28 July 1945.*
Author's collection

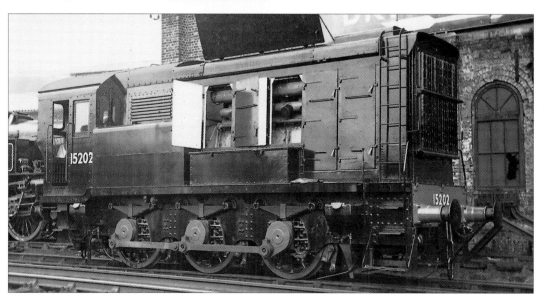

Left: *In October 1948, the first of the three SR prototypes was renumbered into the BR identification system, when Southern No 2 became BR 15202. The locomotive in standard black livery is seen at Brighton, with its roof and side doors open for power unit attention.*
Derek Porter

The Diesel Shunter

Right: *On 9 July 1963, with just over 12 months of operation remaining, No 15203 is seen at Norwood Junction depot. By the time of this illustration, the locomotive was painted in BR green livery and carried a British Railways logo on the side of the fuel tank.* John Scrace

Below: *Although built by the Southern and generally maintained in the old Southern area, the 1959 classified overhaul to No 15203 was undertaken in the Diesel Repair Shops at Stratford on the Eastern Region. This view taken on 16 September 1959, shows the locomotive in dark grey undercoat, awaiting an application of BR green and mechanical completion.* R. W. Dunlop

Right: *The pioneer locomotive of the build No 15201 was looking rather decrepit by mid-1963, painted in locomotive green, this locomotive carried the early style Lion on Wheel logo when photographed broadside at Eastleigh depot on 25 July 1963.* John Scrace

The Diesel Shunter

SR/BR Ashford 0-6-0 diesel-electric 15211-15236 Class 12

Authorised for construction just three years after the SR 0-6-0 prototype units (SR1-3) detailed in the previous section, were eight 0-6-0 standard units under the leadership of the new Southern CME, O. V. S. Bulleid. However, the outbreak of world hostilities in 1939 saw the engineering effort placed on more important items and therefore the eight locos, allocated the numbers Southern 10-18 on official papers of the day were not built. The order was however not cancelled and in 1948 authority was granted for construction of not eight but 26 locos.

As the years had progressed since the original order, so had the design of the standard 0-6-0 locomotive and by the time the 26 SR/BR locomotives were ordered, a true standard design was adopted. However, one very distinguishing feature was the use of Bulleid/Firth-Brown 'Boxpoc' wheels.

All 26 locomotives were constructed at Ashford Works in Kent between 1949 and 1952, and as Bulleid managed to stay on with the Southern Region after nationalisation he was able to oversee the building of 'his' standard 0-6-0 diesel shunter.

The fleet emerged painted in standard black livery offset by white cab side numbers. Initially no BR lion and wheel logo was carried and some examples emerged with numbers applied in white to the red buffer beams.

Although these locomotives did not emerge until the late 1940s and early 1950s, no provision for train braking was made, the only brakes fitted being straight air on the locomotive. This is quite surprising as the fleet had a top speed of $27^1/_2$mph and were destined for trip freight operation.

Allocation of the 26 locomotives was to Norwood Junction and Hither Green, with the fleet to be found operating at all principal yards and stations on the former Southern network. Under BR control, a series of trials were undertaken in the 1950s, which saw one locomotive used on the Western Region in the Bristol area and another as far north as Scotland.

With standardisation being the in word of the mid-1960s, the general decline in freight and wagonload traffic, together with a large surplus of 'standard' 0-6-0 locos, this fleet became redundant from the late 1960s, especially in terms of being non-train brake fitted. locomotives were withdrawn as major failures took them out of traffic in the period 1968-1971, with the final two operational locomotives Nos 15211/2 withdrawn from Norwood in December 1971.

Thankfully one example, No 15224, was saved from the cutters torch and was sold into industrial use in the Kent coalfields. After this work had finished the locomotive was preserved at the Lavender Line and is now at the Spa Valley Railway.

Although none were renumbered into the TOPS system, they were allocated Class 12 in the 1968 programme.

Below: The official portrait view of a Bulleid 'standard' 0-6-0 diesel electric shunting locomotive. This view taken on delivery shows black livery with white running numbers. The number 15212 is also applied in white on the red buffer beam. Note that no BR logo is applied. The' Boxpoc' Bulleid/Firth Brown wheels are clearly visible.
Author's collection

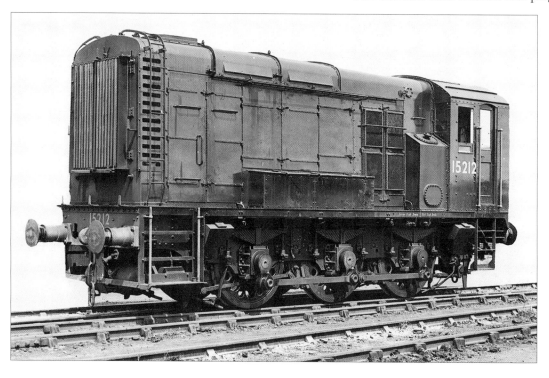

Right: Construction of all 26 members of the fleet was carried out at Ashford Works in Kent, where between late 1948 and January 1952 two bays of the main shop were set aside for the project. Speed of construction varied, with usually four locomotives under assembly at one time. No 15228 is seen in advance stages of assembly in this February 1951 view, some two months before the locomotive was commissioned.
Les Elsey

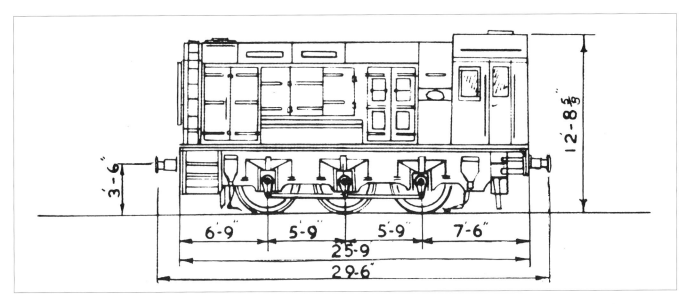

BR 1948 number range:	15211-15236	Cylinder bore:	10in
Former class codes:	D3/13, later 3/9	Cylinder stroke:	12in
Built by:	BR Ashford	Maximum speed:	27$\frac{1}{2}$mph
Years introduced:	1949-1952	Brake type:	Air on locomotive only
Wheel arrangement:	0-6-0	Brake force:	29 tons
Weight:	48 tons	Route availability:	5
Height:	12ft 8$\frac{7}{8}$in	Heating type:	Not fitted
Length:	29ft 6in	Multiple coupling type:	Not fitted
Width:	9ft 0in	Main generator type:	EE801/7D
Wheelbase:	11ft 6in	Traction motor type:	EE506A
Wheel diameter:	4ft 6in	No of traction motors:	2
Min curve negotiable:	4 chains	Gear ratio:	17.5:1
Engine type:	English Electric 6KT	Fuel tank capacity:	660gal
Engine output:	350hp	Cooling water capacity:	140gal
Power at rail:	194hp	Lub oil capacity:	45gal
Tractive effort:	24,600lb	Sanding equipment:	Pneumatic

The Diesel Shunter

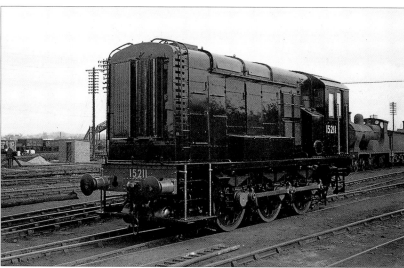

Above: *In all-over black livery with Lion over Wheel bodyside logo No 15219 is seen from its nose end at Hither Green on 27 April 1958. Hither Green and Norwood were the only two official 'sheds' for this fleet when delivered.* Peter Groom

Left: *In pristine ex-works condition, the pioneer member of the fleet, No 15211, is seen in the works yard at Ashford on 23 March 1949.* Peter Metcalf

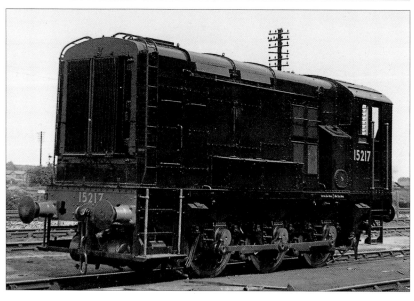

Left: *Another brand new locomotive awaiting delivery from Ashford is No 15217 on 2 July 1949 this locomotive is again in all-over black livery and at this time does not sport a logo.* H. C. Casserley

The Diesel Shunter

Above: *No 15230, painted in BR green livery is seen 'on shed' at Ashford. This locomotive was introduced in September 1951 and allocated to Hither Green, later being transferred to Eastleigh, St Philips Marsh, Bristol, Basingstoke, Fratton before returning to Hither Green for store and withdrawal in 1971.*
John A. M. Vaughan

Below: *Ashford-allocated No 15228 takes a rest between shunting operation, in the yard complex at Ashford, Kent on 19 July 1959. The locomotive is painted in BR black livery, with a good coating of dirt.*
Peter Groom

The Diesel Shunter

Above: Just four years after the picture on page 34 (middle) was taken, the condition of No 15211 had seriously deteriorated. This view from the cab end, showing that no electric marker lights were fitted. The view was taken at New Cross Gate.
Derek Porter

Left: Sporting a pair of traditional Southern white discs, green-liveried No 15231 is seen 'on shed' at Eastleigh on 12 June 1965. At the time, this locomotive had not long been returned to traffic after receiving a full overhaul at Eastleigh Works and a repaint into green livery.
Norman Preedy

Right: Another very clean example of the class, No 15232, again in BR green livery stands outside the front of Eastleigh depot. This locomotive was allocated to Eastleigh in the closing years of steam on the Southern and was frequently photographed by enthusiasts visiting the Hampshire depot to capture the final years and months of steam.
A. D. Mcintyre

Above: *Most of the principal stations on the Southern Region, like the rest of the BR network, had sidings for the off-loading and loading of freight trains. Here at Basingstoke in September 1966, Southern-design 0-6-0 diesel-electric No 15232 shunts a rake of banana vans between Basingstoke depot and the station. This locomotive was introduced in November 1951 and at the time of this illustration was based at Basingstoke shed.*
D. A. Davies

Right: *Looking very tatty in BR green livery, No 15234 is seen parked up in the crane road at Eastleigh depot on 2 November 1968. This locomotive was based at Eastleigh and was withdrawn just three weeks after this picture was taken.*
John Bird

The Diesel Shunter

SR/BR-Paxman 0-6-0 diesel-mechanical 11001

Always a controversial figure, Bulleid and the immediate pre-nationalisation team put forward a one-off 'high-power' diesel-mechanical 0-6-0 locomotive suitable for main line running as well as yard work. It was projected that the locomotive design would be suitable for branch line use on either passenger or freight work.

Given the number 11001 under the BR system, this locomotive was built at the former Southern Railway works at Ashford from 1947, and was therefore a Southern locomotive in most respects, but no records exist as to its projected Southern Railway identity, if indeed one was ever allocated.

According to records the locomotive was 'almost' finished in 1947, but some major parts, likely to have involved the power unit, were delayed. Not emerging until after nationalisation the locomotive came under the remit of R. A. Riddles, the then CME of the BTC who was probably not too amused at having to take delivery of such a one-off, especially as by this time he was fully employed in the LMS design 'standard' shunting locomotive.

When No 11001 emerged in May 1950 it was the most powerful 0-6-0 in the UK and aesthetically looked very pleasing, its total length was 33ft 3in and had a very long low bonnet section. The cab of standard 12ft 11½ height gave excellent all-round visibility for running in either direction and angled forward facing windows improved the visibility over the bonnet. The locomotive was far more conventional in design than previous shunters, having a radiator compartment just reset in from the nose, together with a roof fan. The main power unit, supplied by Paxman-Ricardo was situated over the two leading wheel sets, while the transmission assembly, provided by SSS Powerflow was above the cab-end axle, a large jackshaft and counter weight was located directly below the cab.

After introduction, No 11001 did not have a very happy life. It was deemed too high-geared for shunting work and too low-geared for main line running. Most of its life the locomotive operated from Norwood Junction shed, with some 'main line' turns to Redhill and deployment in Redhill yard. As part of its BR trial period, the locomotive spent a short time working in the Leeds area soon after entry into service.

Sadly after just nine years of work, BR decided the locomotive was non-standard, problematic and costly to maintain and it was subsequently withdrawn on 8 August 1959. It was broken up at Ashford in December 1959.

No 11001 was released from Ashford works in standard BR black livery, a colour it retained all its working life. The locomotive was not fitted with train brake equipment, the only speed retardation being a straight air brake on the locomotive. No electric marker lights were provided, with frontal and rear lighting using oil lamps.

Of course being a true Bulleid design the locomotive was fitted with Bulleid/Firth-Brown 'Boxpoc' wheels.

Right: *In all its ex-works glory No 11001 stands in the works yard at Ashford in May 1950, painted in BR black livery. The unusual design of the forward facing cab windows is visible in this view, which gave footplate staff an improved view ahead of the locomotive.*
Author's collection

BR 1948 number:	11001
Built by:	BR Ashford
Year introduced:	1950
Wheel arrangement:	0-6-0
Weight:	50 tons
Height:	12ft 11½in
Length:	33ft 3in
Width	8ft 7½in
Wheelbase:	12ft 6in
Wheel diameter:	4ft 6in
Min curve negotiable:	4 chains
Engine type:	Paxman Ricardo V12 12RPH
Engine output:	500hp
Power at rail:	410hp
Tractive effort:	33,000lb
Cylinder bore:	7in
Cylinder stroke:	7¾in
Maximum speed:	43½mph
Brake type:	Air on loco, no train brakes

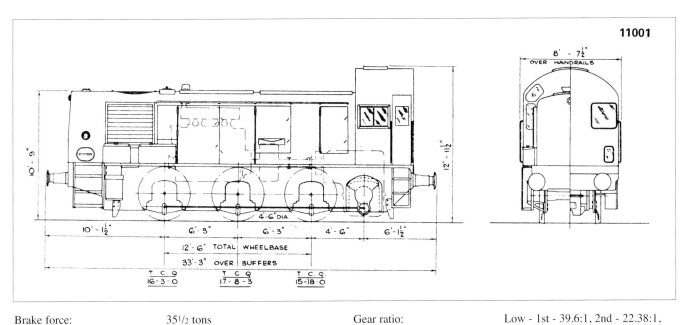

Brake force:	35½ tons	Gear ratio:	Low - 1st - 39.6:1, 2nd - 22.38:1, 3rd - 13.35:1
Route availability:	Not issued		High - 1st - 16.59:1, 2nd - 9.374:1, 3rd - 5.589:1
Heating type:	Not fitted		
Multiple coupling type:	Not fitted		
Transmission	Mechanical	Fuel tank capacity:	606gal
Engine-gearbox —		Cooling water capacity:	60gal
Wellman 'Bibby' coupling		Lub oil capacity:	45gal
Final drive — Powerflow		Sanding equipment:	Pneumatic

Above: *By the middle of 1952 No 11001 was gradually falling from favour on the Southern Region and with other areas of the country trying out diesel shunting traction, the machine was placed on loan to the London Midland Region. It had a period working from Leeds Stourton before moving to Derby where it was eventually stored in mid 1953. The locomotive is seen at Derby Works on 4 September 1953.*
R. J. Buckley

Viewed from its cab end, this illustration shows the very boxy design, with only two small hinged cab windows, neither of which were fitted with an automated wiper. On the buffer beam was just a draw hook, with six lamp brackets for lamps or marker discs. No 11001 is seen at Norwood.
Norman Preedy

Right: *Looking somewhat workstained, Bulleid/Southern Railway 0-6-0 diesel-mechanical, No 11001 is seen at Norwood Junction shed (code 75C), on 23 June 1951, awaiting to depart with a 'trip' working of wooden-sided mineral wagons.*
Brian Morrison

Hibberd 4-wheel diesel-mechanical
11104

This rather unusual locomotive was built in 1950 for the Engineers department, but took a BR standard series running number 11104. The locomotive was a 4-wheel diesel-mechanical and used at West Hartlepool, being renumbered as Departmental 52 in April 1953. In 1965 the locomotive was transferred to the Southern Region at Woking being used for the Bournemouth line electrification project. It was withdrawn and broken up in March 1967.

BR 1948 number:	11104		Power at rail:	39hp
Departmental number:	52		Maximum speed:	15mph
Built by:	Hibberd		Brake type:	Air on loco, no train brakes
Year introduced:	1950		Brake force:	5 tons
Wheel arrangement:	0-4-0		Route availability:	1
Weight:	11 tons		Heating type:	Not fitted
Min curve negotiable:	1 chain		Multiple coupling type:	Not fitted
Engine type:	English National DA4		Transmission type:	Mechanical
Engine output:	52hp		Sanding equipment:	Not fitted

Right: *Painted in black livery, with British Railways in full on the cab side, No 11104 — still to be applied with its number, is seen awaiting delivery to the BTC in the works yard of F. C. Hibberd at Park Royal, London.*
Author's collection

GWR Prototype 0-6-0 diesel-electric GWR 2 15100

The Great Western Railway made their first entry into the 0-6-0 diesel-electric locomotive field in 1933/4, when the company ordered a fully operational locomotive from Hawthorn Leslie of Newcastle. This was to operate alongside GW steam traction for evaluation purposes of the new era in rail freight handling.

The quite heavy machine of what became traditional design weighed in at 51¹/₂ tons and incorporated a standard English Electric six cylinder 6K power unit set to deliver 350hp. The prime mover drove an English Electric generator group which powered EE supplied traction motors.

The locomotive, was delivered to Swindon Works in late 1935, painted in GWR green livery carrying the identity GWR No 2. It took up its first operating allocation at Old Oak Common in April 1936. In comparison with the like period LMS 0-6-0 shunters, GWR No 2 had a much larger fuel supply of 550 gallons, which considerably increased periods between depot visits.

With the outbreak of world hostilities in 1939, the locomotive was earmarked for operation by the War Department, but its call never came, due to the GWR's deployment of the locomotive at a strategic use location - Swansea oil refinery, where it remained until 1946, returning to Old Oak Common for use in the then-massive yard complex at Acton.

Following Nationalisation, the locomotive was given the new BR number of 15100, but in the immediate pre-nationalisation period, the GW formed a new 'diesel' numbering system and GWR No 2 was allocated on paper the identity of GWR 500. Under BR ownership the locomotive was repainted in standard black livery.

The 29ft 0¹/₂in long machine, which it is reported operated well, was fitted with a single driving cab with two operator positions, the locomotive had direct air brakes for its own speed retardation but was not fitted with train vacuum brakes.

In the early 1950s when warning end experiments were being conducted at Swindon Works, No 15100 was repainted with various arrangements of white, light yellow and mid yellow warning panels, stripes and bands, which were the forerunner of the standard 'wasp' warning ends.

No 15100 was re-allocated in 1949 to Weymouth GW but after a few months was returned to Old Oak Common and during the 1950s and early 1960s was used from various depots including Swansea, St Philips Marsh, Swindon and Southall. The locomotive was withdrawn from service at Swindon in May 1965, but remained at Swindon stock shed until October when it was sold to G. Cohen of Morriston, Swansea for scrap. It was disposed of in January 1966.

The principal GW/BTC prototype 0-6-0 did not carry any fixed front or rear end marker lights, but always relied on oil lamps. Access to the power unit control equipment was by six bodyside doors on each side, plus a removable roof section.

A distinguishing feature of this locomotive was the large oval Hawthorn Leslie works plate attached to both sides of the cab.

Below: One of the classic diesel shunting locomotive pictures of all time, Great Western Railway No 2. The locomotive is seen when brand new in the mid 1930s during a demonstration of diesel shunting power in the north-west. It shows lined Great Western green livery. Its structural design is not that far removed from the later BR standard 0-6-0 fleet. **Author's collection**

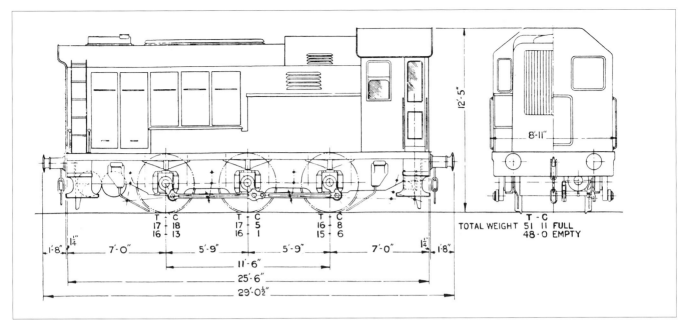

Great Western number:	2		Cylinder bore:	10in
BR 1948 number range:	15100		Cylinder stroke:	12in
Former class codes:	D3/10, later 3/11A		Maximum speed:	19mph
Built by:	Hawthorn Leslie		Brake type:	Air on loco, no train brakes
Year introduced:	1936		Brake force:	31 tons
Wheel arrangement:	0-6-0		Route availability:	Not issued
Weight:	52 tons		Heating type:	Not fitted
Height:	12ft 5in		Multiple coupling type:	Not fitted
Length:	29ft 0½in		Main generator type:	EE
Width	9ft 0in		Aux generator type	EE
Wheelbase:	11ft 6in		Traction motor type:	EE
Wheel diameter:	4ft 0½in		No of traction motors:	2
Min curve negotiable:	3 chains		Gear ratio:	§
Engine type:	English Electric 6KT		Fuel tank capacity:	500gal
Engine output:	350hp		Lub oil capacity:	55gal
Power at rail:	194hp		Sanding equipment:	Pneumatic
Tractive effort:	30,240lb			

Right: *With its five bodyside doors removed, the English Electric 6K power unit is clearly visible. This view shows well the restricted space for working of the prime mover, with fitting staff having to climb inside the framework of the body to gain access to equipment. The roof section also opened to allow the top of the engine to be reached. Note the rather attractive maker's plate attached to the side of the cab.*

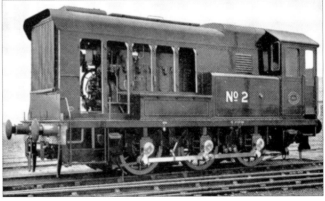

Left: *In later life, the original Great Western prototype was numbered at the start of the GW/BR 0-6-0 locomotive fleet as 15100, being renumbered from GW No 2 in March 1948. On 18 August 1957, the locomotive is seen under repair at Swindon Works, showing BR black livery, Lion over Wheel logo and a white warning end. No 15100 was eventually withdrawn in May 1965.*
Brian Morrison

The Diesel Shunter

GWR/BR 0-6-0 diesel-electric 15101-15107

Although the Great Western Railway was reported to be pleased with their 1935 0-6-0 prototype GWR No 2, it was not until 1945 that the company ordered further like design machines, somewhat surprising, as the GW led the field in diesel passenger railcar development from the 1930s and were always keen on modernisation.

The 1945 order was for seven locos, of the by-now established 'standard' 0-6-0 diesel-electric design. Six of the locomotives were to be powered by the standard English Electric 6K power unit and the seventh (the final locomotive of the order) by Brush/Petter equipment.

In 1945, the Great Western Railway allocated the number range 501-506 to the build, with the contract awarded to GW's own works at Swindon. Assembly of the locomotives was a drawn out affair with the first locomotive not emerging until March 1948, three months after nationalisation, and thus all appeared with BTC five digit shunter series numbers. It is interesting to record that a cast number 502 was applied to the first of the built in 1947 and removed before painting.

Following the 1944 'standard' LMS 0-6-0 shunter design, the GW-built machines had cast number plates on the cab sides rather than painted-on numbers. The fleet also carried GW-style shaded Egyptian slab-serifed letters emblazoning British Railways on the bodysides, complementing the green body paint.

Nos 15101-15106, as the Swindon batch were identified, emerged between March and June 1948 initially working from Swindon before being transferred to Old Oak Common for London area use. From the late 1940s the fleet was transferred to several South Wales locations and by the early 1960s a handful were found operating from London Midland Region depots. All six were withdrawn between 1968-70 and sold for scrap. None were given BR TOPS numbers.

The final locomotive of this group, No 15107, which was built to an almost identical design to the first six and again in the GW factory at Swindon, was a trial of a different power unit/electrical supplier and followed much of the technical design of the LNER prototype No 15004.

No 15107 was built in 1948 and emerged in November 1949 painted in standard BR black livery; this locomotive was in fact the first of the follow-on GW 0-6-0s and was allocated the number 501 in the original series. The locomotive's power unit was a Brush Petter SS4, a two-stroke unit set to deliver 360hp, the output was coupled to a Brush generator group, powering two Brush traction motors.

In common with the original six of the build, cast GW-style numbers were applied and its first allocation was St Philips Marsh, Bristol. The locomotive remained on the Bristol books until early 1957 when it was returned to Swindon Works and stored. The Petter power unit caused major problems. Consideration was given to re-engining with a standard EE unit, but the cost of such an operation was not justified, especially with the mass of standard 0-6-0s then in production. No 15107 was transferred to the Swindon scrap yard and broken up in September 1958.

None of the 15101-15107 build were fitted with train brakes, braking being achieved by a straight air brake on the locomotive and a parking brake.

Below: This amazing line up of shunting motive power was for the official English Electric photographer at Acton Yard in West London in 1954, and shows three eras of shunting power. On the left is Great Western 'Pannier' No 8770. In the centre is Great Western-ordered 0-6-0 diesel-electric No 15103 complete with its cast number plate in true Great Western tradition, while on the right is BR standard 0-6-0 No 13030, a locomotive delivered new to Old Oak Common on 5 October 1953. **Author's collection**

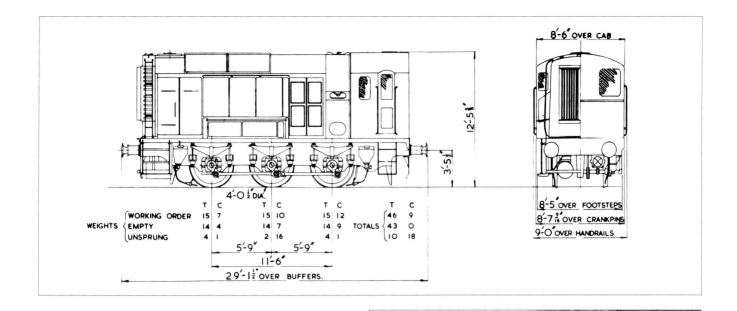

Right: Although ordered by the Great Western Railway, the six 'production GW shunters' were not delivered until after Nationalisation, and thus carried British Railways branding and numbers from delivery. In green livery, with British Railways in full on the body side and a painted number on the red buffer beam, No 15102 is seen when new attached to a Great Western shunting truck at Acton in May 1948.
Author's collection

Great Western number range:	502, -	501 (not carried)
BR 1948 number range:	15101-15106	15107
Former class codes:	D3/11, later 3/11	-
Built by:	BR Swindon	BR Swindon
Years introduced:	1948	1949
Wheel arrangement:	0-6-0	0-6-0
Weight:	47 tons	46 tons
Height:	12ft 5⁵/₈in	12ft 5¹/₂in
Length:	29ft 1¹/₂in	29ft 0¹/₂in
Width:	9ft 0n	9ft 0in
Wheelbase:	11ft 6in	11ft 6in
Wheel diameter:	4ft 0¹/₂in	4ft 0¹/₂in
Min curve negotiable:	3¹/₂ chains	3 chains
Engine type:	English Electric 6K	Brush Petter SS4
Engine output:	350hp	360hp
Power at rail:	194hp	220hp
Tractive effort:	33,500lb	33,500lb
Cylinder bore:	10in	§
Cylinder stroke:	12in	§
Maximum speed:	20mph	20mph
Brake type:	Air on loco, no train brakes	Air on loco, no train brakes
Brake force:	27 tons	27 tons
Route availability:	Not issued	Not issued
Heating type:	Not fitted	Not fitted
Multiple coupling type:	Not fitted	Not fitted
Main generator type:	EE801B	Brush
Aux generator type	EE	Brush
Traction motor type:	EE506B	Brush
No of traction motors:	2	2
Gear ratio:	21.7:1	§
Fuel tank capacity:	659gal	600gal
Cooling water capacity:	140gal	150gal
Lub oil capacity:	65gal	55gal
Sanding equipment:	Pneumatic	Pneumatic

The Diesel Shunter

Above: *Looking every bit a 'standard' 0-6-0 diesel-electric shunting loco, the first of the build No 15101 is seen at Swindon Works posing for its official works picture. The livery is locomotive green, with full shadow BR legend on the body side doors. Note the depot code of PDN, indicating Paddington, on the running plate.* Author's collection

Left: *Although carrying a cast GW-style number plate, No 15107 did not emerge from Swindon until November 1949 and was finished in BR black livery. This official works picture of the locomotive shows a rather over-size Lion over Wheel logo on the engine room door.* Author's collection

The Diesel Shunter

Above: *Looking rather grubby, mainly ingrained with brake dust, and the signs of a fuel spill down the fuel tank, No 15101 is seen at Acton on 31 August 1948. It just goes to show how quickly such a workhorse became discoloured.* C. C. B. Herbert

Above: *Looking more like modern day graffiti on the cab end, for some reason the fact that this locomotive was No 2 (or 15102) appeared to be important, as its identity is scrawled on the cab end and highlighted on the cast plate and buffer beam. No 15102 is seen at Cardiff East Dock in mid-1961.* R. S. Ford

Right: *By the mid-1960s standardisation was being applied to the pre-Nationalisation shunter fleet. With the cast number plate removed and the identity of No 15102 applied by transfer, the locomotive is seen derelict at Derby Locomotive Works on 21 March 1968. By the summer of the same year the locomotive had been sold to the Steelbreaking & Dismantling Co of Chesterfield.* P. I. Allan

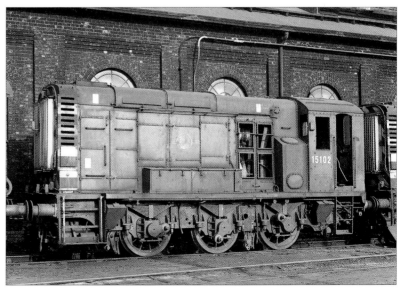

LNER/BR 0-6-0 diesel-electric prototypes
LNER 8000-8003
15000-15003

In 1944, at the same time as the London Midland & Scottish Railway was introducing its 'standard' shunting locomotive design, the London & North Eastern was building a batch of four 0-6-0 standard-outline locomotives at the time destined for use in Temple Mills and Goodmayes Yards, London.

Built by Doncaster Works, the locomotives followed the by-then standard outline, but incorporated a few slightly different features. The buffer beams were quite shallow, while the cabs were slightly larger than LMS designs. Revisions were also made to bodyside ventilation and access doors. To improve yard operation the coupled wheelbase was also extended to 11ft 9in.

The design weighed in at 51 tons and carried fuel tanks of 580 gallons, this equating to up to 28 days yard work without refuelling.

As the design was intended for work in busy yards, it was agreed from the outset to install train braking, this was done using the standard vacuum system. Electric front and rear marker lights were also fitted from new.

The first locomotive of the build, LNER No 8000, was completed at Doncaster in July 1944, being used as the works pilot until allocated to Stratford a few weeks later. The second of the build followed in August 1944 and was demonstrated at a press launch at Liverpool Street in September. Delays in delivery of the power units and control equipments saw the final two locomotives stored after initial construction, not entering service until 1945.

After about a year of operation in the East London area, all four locomotives were transferred to March, Whitemoor Yard. The fleet remained working here until the 1960s when they were transferred to the London Midland Region.

By 1967/8 the fleet was deemed as 'non-standard' and all were withdrawn for scrap. At the time of the initial contract, five locomotives were ordered, but the fifth example, allocated the number 8004, was transferred to Brush after its frames had been laid (see next section).

Under LNER the locomotives were numbered 8000-8003, under BR ownership from January 1948 this was amended to the standard diesel shunter series as 15000-15003, but renumbering was not completed until the early 1950s.

In terms of livery, the locomotives were initially finished in LNER or NE black livery, with a Doncaster oval works plate attached to the nose end engine room door. Under BR control, the black livery was retained, with initially the Lion on Wheel emblem applied, this later gave way to the standard BR logo. Repaints in the 1960s saw standard BR locomotive green applied. No examples survived to be painted in BR blue or receive TOPS classification.

It is interesting to note how pre-nationalisation variations remained even after the formation of the BR for when locomotives of this fleet were repainted and renumbered in the BR system, all had their number applied on the main bodyside in true LNER style.

Below: Although built by the LNER, when the first of the four 0-6-0 shunters emerged from Doncaster Works in July 1944 it was painted in all-over black livery with NE branding on the body side panelling, the running number was applied below. This broadside view in the works yard at Doncaster was taken prior to the locomotive entering traffic at Stratford that August. While at Doncaster the locomotive was used as works pilot to 'run-in' the power unit and control equipment.
Author's collection

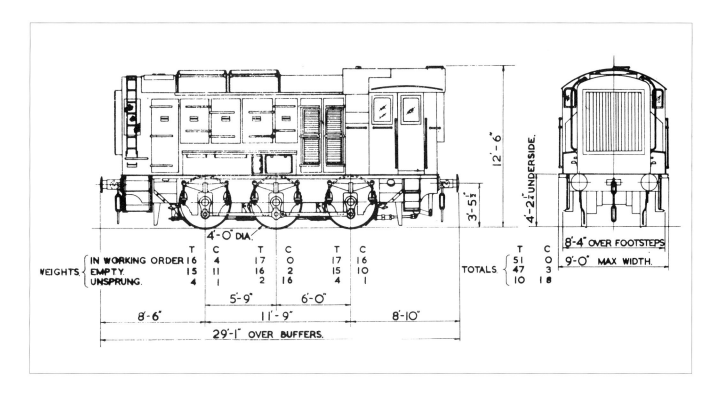

LNER number range:	8000-8003	Cylinder bore:	10in
BR 1948 number range:	15000-15003	Cylinder stroke:	12in
Former class codes:	DEJ-1, D3/9, later 3/10	Maximum speed:	20mph
Built by:	LNER Doncaster	Brake type:	Air on loco, vacuum for train
Year introduced:	1944	Brake force:	32 tons
Wheel arrangement:	0-6-0	Route availability:	Not issued
Weight:	51 tonnes	Heating type:	Not fitted
Height:	12ft 6¹/₈in	Multiple coupling type:	Not fitted
Length:	29ft 1in	Main generator type:	Brush
Width	9ft 0in	Aux generator type:	Brush
Wheelbase:	11ft 9in	Traction motor type:	Brush
Wheel diameter:	4ft 0¹/₂in	No of traction motors:	2
Min curve negotiable:	3 chains	Gear ratio:	21.7:1
Engine type:	English Electric 6RKT	Fuel tank capacity:	580gal
Engine output:	350hp	Cooling water capacity	140gal
Power at rail:	200hp	Lub oil capacity:	75gal
Tractive effort:	32,000lb	Sanding equipment:	Pneumatic

Right: *This picture dated 11 November 1944 shows the second of the Doncaster build, No 8001 in the Works yard at Doncaster. This locomotive had a very slightly different water gutter on the cab roof, with a down guide at the cab end, this followed water running down onto staff using the door. No 8001 shows the main doors and inspection covers open, giving access to the English Electric prime mover, generator group (left) and radiator assembly (right). This locomotive was, at the date of this picture, allocated to Stratford, but was returned to Doncaster for power unit attention.*
Author's collection

The Diesel Shunter

Left: *These were some of the earliest 'standard' design shunting locomotives to be equipped with vacuum train brake equipment. The control pipe can be seen mounted on the buffer beam with the hose attached to the front end below the left side of the radiator. No 8003 is seen at Whitemoor Yard, March in August 1946.*
Author's collection

Below: *By the time this illustration was taken, on 4 October 1958, the pioneer locomotive of the fleet had been given a classified overhaul at BR Derby works and repainted in full BR locomotive green with Lion over Crown logo on the battery box side.* R. Jackson

Below: *Even with a small fleet of locos, which it might be assumed would be painted from the same chart, livery differences are to be found. Nos 15000 and 15001, seen here at March depot in July 1952, are both painted in black livery, but the numbers and Lion over Wheel crests are in different positions.*
R. Wells

The Diesel Shunter

Above & Left: *Two views of No 15002, introduced in December 1944. The illustration above shows the locomotive in BR black livery with the Lion over Wheel logo on the cab side. The view left, taken at March in April 1959 shows the locomotive in green livery with the later design Lion over Crown British Railways logo. By this time, some form of warning end had been applied, visible within the front end radiator.*
Derek Porter/Peter Groom

Right: *Taken in almost the identical location to the illustration left, No 15001 is again seen basking outside March shed in Cambridgeshire while taking a rest between duties in Whitemoor yard. Dated 18 June 1958, the locomotive shows standard BR locomotive green livery with conventional BR logo on the battery box.*
P. J. Sharpe

The Diesel Shunter

LNER/BR 0-6-0 diesel-electric prototype 15004

The Brush Company, based in Loughborough, followed closely the development work on diesel shunting power during the 1930s, especially that performed by the LMSR using English Electric traction. Records show that if the outbreak of War had not happened in 1939, a prototype Brush locomotive was on the cards, as the company was looking at ways of expanding rail operations to supplement their trolley-bus business.

Following the return to normality in the mid-1940s, the plan to design and build a Brush diesel shunter was again considered. At this time, the Chairman of Brush was Sir Ronald Matthews, who was also the Chairman of the London & North Eastern Railway. Through this association, Brush entered into a deal with the LNER to develop a trial 360hp diesel-electric locomotive.

The locomotive, of basically traditional design and following the style of the 1944 Doncaster-built locomotives Nos 8000-8003, was part-assembled in terms of frame members and some mechanical sections, at the LNER works in Doncaster, before being taken to the Loughborough factory of Brush for completion. The locomotive emerged in September 1947, being allocated the LNER identity of 8004, but this was not carried.

The locomotive was fitted with a Brush/Petter SS4 engine, a two-stroke unit set to deliver 360hp. Coupled to this was a Brush generator group which provided power to two Brush traction motors. The machine had a top operating speed of 22mph.

The locomotive was initially used at the Brush 'Falcon' works for development work, moving on to by then BR metals the following year at Temple Mills and March, but was still un-numbered. Its trials and development status, saw it return to the Brush factory at the end of 1948 after a successful period of testing. Following a classified overhaul, the locomotive was 'sold' to the BTC and was taken into BR stock in April 1949 at March. Over the next 13 years the locomotive was deployed at several Eastern Region depots, before ending its career at New England (Peterborough) in October 1962. After transfer to Doncaster Works, the locomotive was withdrawn and disposed of for scrap at Doncaster the following year.

Although a 'one-off' example, No 15004 operated well, having frequent visits to Derby Works (close to Loughborough) but the trial was generally deemed as a success.

When originally constructed, this prototype was finished in grey workshop primer, this being carried during its initial private-ownership trial period. After being taken into BR stock it was repainted into standard black livery, offset by its running number applied to the bodyside engine compartment doors. The locomotive was later repainted into BR green. In the 1950s, the locomotive was used in the development of high-visibility warning ends, with a white and black horizontal band pattern applied to the cab end.

To allow shunting of heavy trains and as part of its development role, the locomotive was built with vacuum train brake equipment, using a straight air system on the locomotive. No electric front or rear lights were fitted.

Below: Built by Brush Loughborough and LNER/BR Doncaster this trial locomotive emerged after nationalisation in December 1948 and thus assumed its BR number 15004. Looking very similar to the previously-detailed fleet, the sole example of this class is seen at New England shed, Peterborough on 15 May 1960, painted in BR black livery. A number of detail structural differences existed between this locomotive and the previous examples, to accommodate the Brush/Petter power unit. **Peter Hanson**

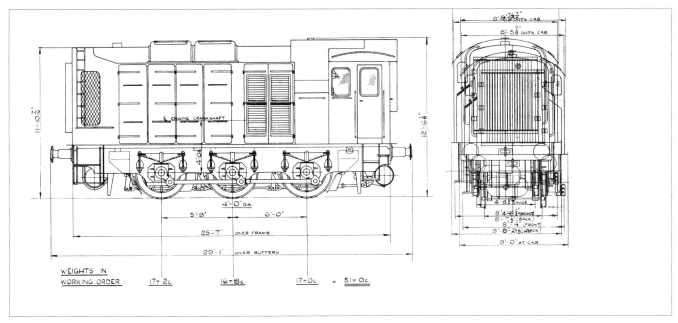

BR 1948 number range:	15004	Cylinder bore:	§
Former class codes:	DEJ-2, D3/14, later 3/2	Cylinder stroke:	§
Built by:	Brush, Loughborough	Maximum speed:	22mph
Year built:	1947	Brake type:	Air on loco, vacuum for train
Year introduced:	1949	Brake force:	36 tons
Wheel arrangement:	0-6-0	Route availability:	Not issued
Weight:	51 tons	Heating type:	Not fitted
Height:	12ft 6¹/sin	Multiple coupling type:	Not fitted
Length:	29ft 1in	Main generator type:	Brush
Width	9ft 0in	Aux generator type	Brush
Wheelbase:	11ft 9in	Traction motor type:	Brush
Wheel diameter:	4ft 0 in	No of traction motors:	2
Min curve negotiable:	3¹/2 chains	Gear ratio:	§
Engine type:	Brush/Petter SS4	Fuel tank capacity:	660gal
Engine output:	360hp	Cooling water capacity	120gal
Power at rail:	230hp	Lub oil capacity:	45gal
Tractive effort:	32,000lb	Sanding equipment:	Pneumatic

Left: *The cab end of No 15004 was considerably different from the previous design, with a large protruding section between the cab end windows, housing control equipment accessed from within the cab. Sporting a white warning end arrangement, No 15004 is seen at New England.*
Geoff Silcock

Right: *No 15004 was used mainly in the Peterborough and March areas from its introduction in April 1949 until withdrawn on 5 October 1962, its work being taken over by deliveries of 'standard' BR design 0-6-0 diesel-electric units. After a period in store at Doncaster the locomotive was cut up at the works in mid-1963.*
P. W. Wells

LMS/English Electric 0-6-0 diesel-electric LMS 7120-7131, 12033-12138 Class 11

This fleet of LMS shunters was the culmination of the many trial and test locomotives of the LMSR in the 1930s and can be described as a true wartime design.

Its design, which later formed the basis for the UK standard 0-6-0 diesel-electric shunting loco, was a development of the previous LMS 0-6-0 diesel-electric builds and incorporated the proven English Electric 6K power unit, but used the two traction motor outside frame arrangement rather than the then recently tried 'jackshaft' drive system, which at the time was suffering from frame fractures. The successful design development of this fleet followed refining of the double reduction gears which reduced overheating.

The first locomotive of the build, painted in LMS black and numbered LMS 7120 emerged in 1944 and was indeed a very historic moment as this was the first of well over 1,000 locomotives of a like design to emerge for UK mainline operation and was the design 'base' for many other fleets of locomotives for the UK and European operation as well as the War Department (later MoD).

The first order for the design was for 20 locomotives and after ordering were directed to WD use, but while under construction, the final six locomotives were deemed not required and went to the LMS. Various repeat orders were placed by the LMS and indeed by BR after Nationalisation, and by 1952 when the order books were closed a fleet of 106 locomotives was in service. In addition to the LMS factory at Derby, examples had been built to the LMS drawings, at Darlington for LNER-area deployment.

Soon after Nationalisation it was announced that the design of this fleet would be developed into a 'new' standard diesel-electric shunting loco, which was refined by Chief Engineer R. A. Riddles.

The external design of the locomotives has a full width cab at one end, with driving positions either side of a central control desk. The driving controls were suitable for operation in either direction from the same position. Visibility from the cab end was good, but for forward operation the vision along the side of the engine room was no better than on a steam locomotive. Forward from the cab was an electrical compartment, the main power unit bay and at the nose end, the cooler group.

Front end equipment was basic, with just buffers and a screw shackle on the draw bar, no train braking was provided, locomotive speed reduction was achieved by a direct air brake system.

When built the first 12 locomotives emerged with LMS numbering 7120-7131, while the remainder took the five digit BR 'modern traction' series in the 12045-12138 range, the original 12 being renumbered into the series as 12033-12044. Some members of the fleet remained in traffic long enough to see a TOPS numeric classification given to the fleet — Class 11, however none remained in service long enough to be given a five digit class prefixed number.

Following the original black livery with bodyside mounted Lion on Wheel crest, the fleet was repainted into BR standard green livery with the later BR Lion over Crown crest. A handful of locomotives remained in traffic long enough to be repainted into corporate BR rail blue with yellow/black wasp ends.

From new, electric front and rear marker lights were installed, which were fitted with a white element over which a red shade could be added for rear-end use. One important structural change to befall the class was the removal of the nose end side ladders to reach the top of the radiator, which followed overhead electrification of the LNW route.

Left: *Painted in LMS livery and numbered 7120, this was the first of the 1944-design LMS standard diesel-electric 0-6-0 locomotives. The design was the culmination of all the prototype designs and trials. No 7120 entered service in May 1945 and continued in traffic until January 1969. Under BTC numbering the locomotive became 12033 from July 1948 and eventually became part of BR Class 11.* **Author's collection**

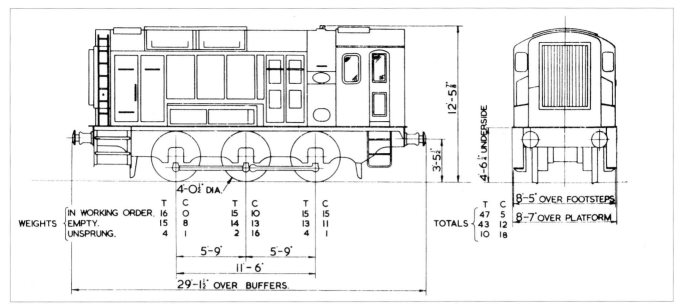

		T	**C**		
				T	**C**
WEIGHTS	IN WORKING ORDER. 16	O	15 10	15 15	
	EMPTY. 15	8	14 13	13 11	
	UNSPRUNG. 4	1	2 16	4 1	

	T	**C**
TOTALS	47	5
	43	12
	10	18

4'-0½" DIA.
5'-9" 5'-9"
11'-6"
29'-1½" OVER BUFFERS.
12'-5⅞"
3'-5½"
4'-6¼" UNDERSIDE
8'-5" OVER FOOTSTEPS
8'-7" OVER PLATFORM

LMS number range:	7120-7131	Brake force:	29 tons
BR 1948 number range:	12033-12138	Route availibility:	5
Former class codes:	DEJ 3, later D3/8, D3/8A	Heating type:	Not fitted
Built by:	LMS/BR Derby, BR Darlington	Multiple coupling type:	Not fitted
Years introduced:	1945-1952	Main generator type:	EE
Wheel arrangement:	0-6-0	Aux generator type	EE
Weight:	48 tons	Traction motor type:	EE
Height:	12ft 5⅞in	No of traction motors:	2
Length:	29ft 1½in	Gear ratio:	21.7:1
Width :	8ft 7in	Fuel tank capacity:	659gal
Wheelbase:	11ft 6in	Cooling water capacity:	140gal
Wheel diameter:	4ft 0½in	Lub oil capacity:	12033-12048 - 65gal `
Min curve negotiable:	3½ chains		12049-12138 - 45gal
Engine type:	English Electric 6KT	Sanding equipment:	Pneumatic
Engine output:	350hp		
Power at rail:	194hp		
Tractive effort:	35,000lb		
Cylinder bore:	10in		
Cylinder stroke:	12in		
Maximum speed:	20mph		
Brake type:	Air on loco, vacuum on train		

Below: *A truly amazing picture taken inside the main erecting shop at Derby Works on 14 August 1947 shows six of the LMS design of 'standard' 0-6-0 diesel-electric locomotives under construction.*
Author's collection

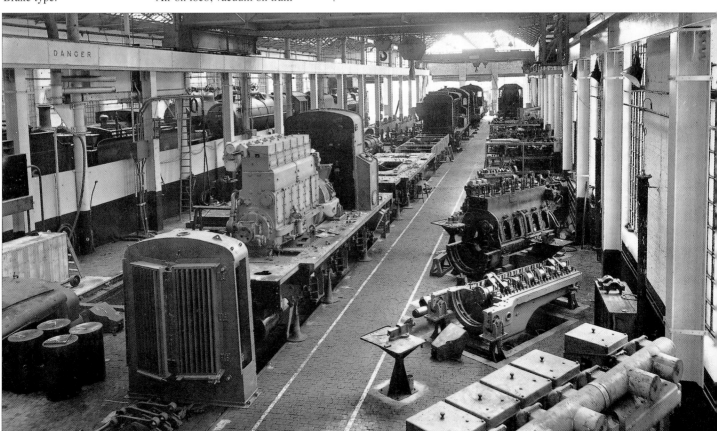

Above: *The first of the Darlington-built locomotives No 12103 is viewed from the cab end, showing that no train brake equipment was installed and no windscreen wipers. Two electric marker lights were provided.*
Derek Porter

Right: *Another brand new Darlington product, No 12125 is seen in the works yard on 11 October 1952 awaiting testing and delivery to King's Cross (Top Shed). The locomotive sports black livery with a red buffer beam, front end illumination consists of two marker lights on the body panelling just above the buffer beam.*
A. Ellis

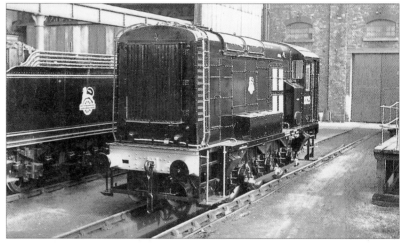

Left: *Looking rather tatty, No 12099 is seen at Willesden in February 1958. this locomotive was built in March 1952 and had at this time not received a classified overhaul or repaint since introduction. No 12099 was eventually repainted into BR green and remained in service until July 1971.*
M. Peachey

The Diesel Shunter

This page: *Considerable efforts were made from the early-1960s to introduce an end-warning system to shunting locos, it was eventually agreed that a yellow/black chevron style paint scheme would be applied. This did give notice to staff that it was a traction unit but the omission of a high power headlight or other warning factor did little to tell staff a train was approaching. These two views of No 12100 at Willesden show BR green livery complete with wasp warning ends. The locomotive is involved with hump operations. The use of a non-brake-fitted locomotive on such operations was of little consequence, as to perform hump operations the brake pipes were disconnected.* Both: **Author's collection**

The Diesel Shunter

Left: *After working in the Derby area from construction in 1952 until 1957, No 12100 was transferred to Willesden, where it remained working until March 1962 when it was transferred to the Liverpool area. While allocated to 1A, No 12100 is seen at Stratford in January 1960 awaiting repairs at the Diesel Repair Shop (DRS).*
M. Williams

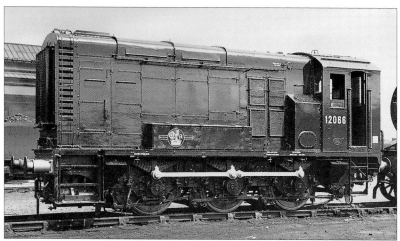

Right & Below: *The two locomotives illustrated here clearly demonstrate how different workshops applied what was designed as a standard livery, in two totally different styles. On the right No 12066 is seen in BR green livery at Derby Works in July 1958 with the Lion over Crown emblem on the battery box side at the radiator end, while the illustration below of No 12063 at Stratford in 1960 shows the more conventional positioning of the emblem on the engine room side doors. Records show No 12066 was repainted at Derby Works and No 12063 at Stratford Works.*
R. J. Buckley/R. E. Vincent

The Diesel Shunter

Right: *Some of the Class 11 fleet were taken over by industrial operators when withdrawn by BR. One such locomotive was No 12122, sold to the National Coal Board in 1971 and moved to South Wales. After a couple of years work it sustained serious nose end collision damage at the Lion Disposal Point near Blaenavon and was eventually taken to Crigglestonewhere it was disposed of at British Oak in 1985. The locomotive is seen at Lion Disposal Point near Blaenavon.*
Graham Scott-Lowe

Below: *This locomotive is not quite what it seems. No 7120 on the preserved Lakeside & Haverthwaite Railway (LHR) in Cumbria is in fact a locomotive of LMS design which was built at Derby Locomotive Works for War Department service. It was constructed in 1945 and spent most of its working life at Longmoor, Bicester, Shoeburyness and Welford before being withdrawn from Bicester as AD601 in 1980. It was then sold to the LHR which has completely rebuilt the locomotive and given it the number of the first example of the LMS Fairburn design. It now has one or two additions to its original design, vacuum braking and a roof height headlight on the cab end.* Chris Dixon

The Diesel Shunter

BR Swindon and Doncaster 0-6-0 diesel-mechanical D2000-D2199/D2370-D2399 Class 03 03004-03399

After dozens of 'small' shunting locomotives had been built, by a variety of different manufacturers, BR tried, perhaps rather late in the day, to establish a standard small medium-wheelbase, 0-6-0 design, fitted with a diesel-mechanical transmission.

The locomotive design adopted incorporated the best of all the 'short-run' fleets, in terms of equipment design, positioning and looks, and incorporated the well proven and highly reliable Gardner 8L3 prime mover, set to deliver 204bhp. Transmission was provided by a Wilson-Drewry CA5 R7 forward and reverse gearbox. In many ways the design was a refinement of the slightly earlier Drewry Car Co built 0-6-0 diesel-mechanical fleet, covered in the next section.

Construction contracts for the small standard BR 0-6-0 was placed in late 1955 with the BR Workshops Division, who contracted the mechanical assembly to Swindon and Doncaster Works. A total of 230 locomotives were being built in a period from December 1957 to June 1962. Swindon Works was given the initial build contract, and long prior to the emergence of the first loco, the Works Manager announced the fleet would carry steam locomotive style chimneys, and in true Great Western workshop tradition would have a copper cap! When BR got wind of such a plan, a directive was soon issued on exhaust stack design, which was to be of the conical or 'saxa' style. Swindon Works did actually have the last laugh on this subject, as after the fleet was introduced, the light weight at the nose end caused adhesion problems. The answer lay in the fitting of a 'plant-pot' surround to the exhaust stack, which was actually cast from heavy metal to a steam locomotive design — albeit without a copper cap.

The driving cab design of this fleet was probably the best of all the small 0-6-0s, with good size cab doors, and an excellent visibility from the greenhouse style windows. The structural design of the body section consisted of five removable side panels on each side to give access to the engine and equipment bay. The section closest to the cab was of slightly raised height.

When ordered the 1948 'modern traction' numbering system was still in use, and the range 11187 onwards was allocated. However, while assembly was being carried out the 1957 numeric series using a four figure 'D' prefixed number was introduced and the new design was issued with the D2000 series, which was carried from new. As the fleet eventually rose to 230 members with several follow on orders, the number range went right through the D20xx and D21xx series. As the D22xx series was already allocated elsewhere, this fleet was continued in the D2370-D2399 range.

The entire fleet emerged in standard BR locomotive green, and as the yellow/black wasp stripe ends design was standardised, these were applied from new to later-built locomotives and retro-applied to earlier builds. From 1967 repaints following overhaul were carried out in standard BR corporate rail blue, again with yellow/black wasp stripe ends.

From 1973, following the introduction of five-digit, class-prefixed TOPS numbering, the fleet was identified as Class 03 and renumbered in the 03xxx range. By this time a number of locomotives had been withdrawn, so in this range a number of gaps were found, as no attempt was made to close up the range, as was the case in some classes.

Two locomotives of special interest are No D2370/1, which were constructed to the standard design as Departmental Nos 91 and 92 for Eastern Region use. The pair were however renumbered into the main fleet in mid-1967.

Although 230 locomotives were constructed, a fleet of this size was soon found to far exceed the needs of the rail industry, which was rapidly closing freight yards and removing the very work for which this and other small fleets were assembled. A number of locomotives were withdrawn from the mid-1960s, with a large number passing to industrial users. The fleet remained operating for the mainstream railway through to 2003, with one example remaining in use as the depot pilot at Hornsey EMU depot in North London. This example, No 03179, now carries West Anglia Great Northern (WAGN) livery.

Many of the withdrawn Class 03s have also found their way into preservation, where their design, basic engineering and flexibility have been very useful to a number of preserved railways.

Vacuum train brakes were applied from new. With the onset of air braking through the 1960s and 1970s a large number of locomotives were fitted with dual air/vacuum brake equipment, with some fitted with high-level waist-height air connections for coupling to EMU stock not fitted with buffer beam level connections.

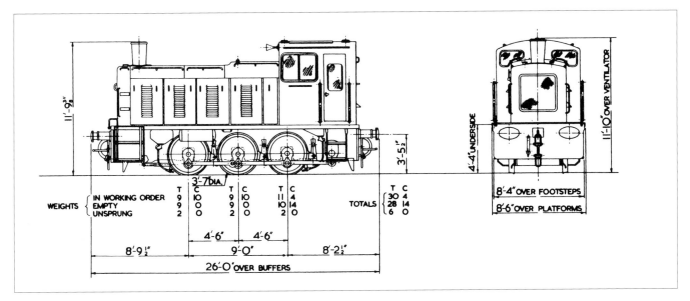

WEIGHTS		T	C	T	C	T	C		T	C
	IN WORKING ORDER	9	10	9	9	11	4	TOTALS	30	4
	EMPTY	9	10	9	10	10	14		28	14
	UNSPRUNG	9	2	9	2	10	2		6	0

TOPS number range:	03004-03399
Original 1948 number range:	11187-11211 (not carried)
1957 BR number range:	D2000-D2199, D2370-D2399
Former class codes:	DJ15, then D2/2, 2/1
Built by:	BR workshops Swindon and Doncaster
Years introduced:	1957-1962
Wheel arrangement:	0-6-0
Weight:	30.3 tons
Height:	12ft 3^{7}/16in. Note: 1
Length:	26ft 0in
Width:	8ft 6in
Wheelbase:	9ft 0in
Wheel diameter:	3ft 7in
Min curve negotiable:	2 chains
Engine type:	Gardner 8L3
Engine output:	204hp
Power at rail:	152hp
Tractive effort:	5,300lb
Cylinder bore:	5^{1}/2in
Cylinder stroke:	7^{3}/4in
Maximum speed:	28^{1}/2mph
Brake type:	Vacuum, some rebuilt with dual
Brake force:	13 tons
Route availability:	1

Heating type:	Not fitted
Multiple coupling type:	Not fitted Note: 1
Transmission:	Engine-gearbox — Fluidrive type 23 HYD
	Final drive — SCG RF11
Gear ratio:	First - 4.07:1
	Second - 2.33:1
	Third - 1.55:1
	Fourth - 1:1
	Fifth - 1:1.87
Fuel tank capacity:	300gal
Cooling water capacity:	40gal
Lub oil capacity:	8gal
Sanding equipment:	Pneumatic

Notes

1: Nos D2119/20/41/2/4/5/51/2 (03119/20/41/2/4/5/51/2) rebuilt with 6in lower cab for BPGV line operation and fitted with multiple operation equipment

One locomotive remains in TOC operation, No 03179 at WAGN's Hornsey depot. Several locomotives are in industrial use and in preservation.

Left: Released from Swindon Works just prior to Christmas 1957, the first of the BR 'standard' small 204hp diesel-mechanical shunters No D2000 in BR green livery is seen at Hatfield on the Eastern Region on 12 April 1958. **Ian McIntosh**

Right: With its early 'Saxa' style exhaust stack, all over green-liveried No D2001 is viewed from its nose end in mid-1958 resting between duties at Hitchin. As can be seen from the buffer beam, vacuum train brakes were fitted to this design from new, together with windscreen wipers and electric end marker lights. **T. Lawrence**

The Diesel Shunter

Left: *The Gardner 8L3 engine and transmission system on this design was accessed via four removable side inspection doors, each of which has angled side grilles to provide some form of ventilation to the engine. No D2002 (note the dot between the D and number) is seen at Hitchin soon after delivery in January 1958.*
F. W. Day

Below: *To overcome a slight lack of adhesion at the nose end, a heavyweight collar was placed around the exhaust stack on later-built locos, very much resembling a steam locomotive chimney. No D2120 is seen outside Swindon shed in October 1959.*
P. J. Thomas

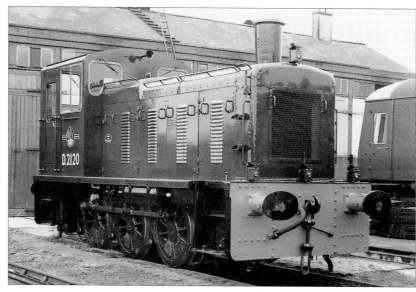

Below: *This illustration of No D2122 at Swindon Stock Shed on 1 November 1959 has been included as the low sunlight shows up much of the underframe equipment, and should be a considerable help to model makers. It will also be noted that the cast oval works plate is attached to the bonnet section just in front of the cab, this has a locomotive green background and polished letters and edge. No D2122 was a Western Region locomotive allocated to Danygraig, Swansea.*
J. C. Haydon

The Diesel Shunter

Above: *It was not often that members of this fleet were given passenger workings. However, on 12 September 1959 No D2017 was entrusted with a Railway Club special, seen at Bartlow en route to Saffron Walden.* John Faulkner

Right: *With the number A211V cast into its chimney, June 1959 built No D2087 is seen shunting stock at Swindon Works on 22 August of the same year.* J. Bucknell

Below: *Looking rather weather worn, No D2007 is seen shunting a long freight train at Bury St Edmunds in mid-1962. At this time the locomotive was allocated to Cambridge depot.* John C. Baker

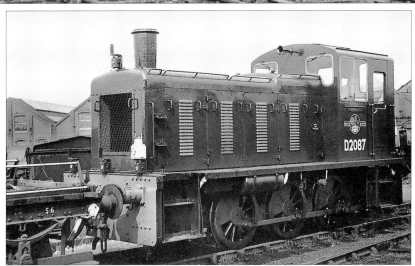

Left: *With a white disc on the nose end, a trademark of the Southern Region, No D2083 introduced in March 1959 and always allocated to the Southern Region until withdrawal in June 1969, is seen at Eastleigh. This locomotive is one of the class which did not remain in traffic long enough to be renumbered into the five-digit TOPS system from mid-1973.*
P. J. Sharpe

Right: *Built at Swindon Works in May 1961, No D2194 is seen in ex-shops condition a few days after release from the works test area. This locomotive was allocated new to Swindon, moving to Worcester shed at the end of 1966. Coupled back to back with No D2194 is No D2146, another Swindon product which emerged in February 1961 and was also allocated to Swindon. Both locomotives show standard BR green livery with full 'wasp' yellow and black warning ends.* J. Loader

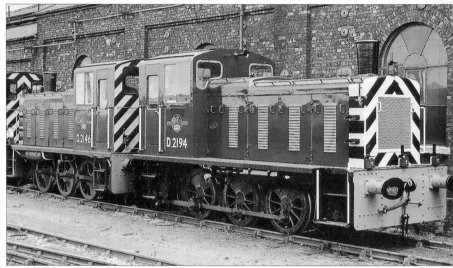

Below: *Another Swindon product, No D2183 in immaculate condition before taking up duty. Note that even the buffers have yet to become marked, in this March 1962 picture.*
M. Edwards

The Diesel Shunter

Right: The orders placed for the BR 'standard' small 0-6-0 diesel-mechanical shunter exceeded the original expectations of the railway's engineering arm, to the extent that the number range originally allocated in the D20xx and D21xx series was insufficient for the total order size. This problem was answered by allocating the series D2370-D2399. No D2388 is illustrated, a Doncaster built example which entered traffic in April 1961 at Birkenhead. On 27 July 1963, the locomotive is seen performing station shunting duties at Chester.
Brian Stephenson

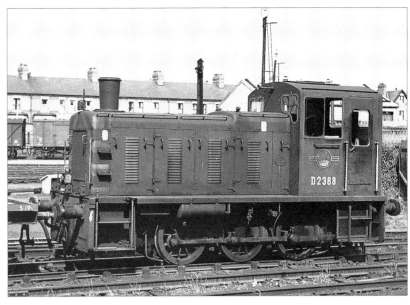

Left: Locomotives D2370/1 were originally Departmental Engineers locomotives Nos 91 and 92, being introduced in June and July 1958. The pair were identical to the production small 0-6-0 diesel-mechanical shunter, and when their life in the engineering division was completed, the pair were absorbed into the main fleet, taking the two vacant 'slots' in the number range below the final batch. No D2371 painted in standard BR green livery with wasp nose end but retaining its original 'Saxa' exhaust stack, is seen at Cambridge on 29 July 1967, a couple of days after being renumbered from Departmental No 92.
D. Hepworth

Below: With the word 'scrap' chalked on the body side, new No D.2126 poses on Swindon shed in January 1960, when just four weeks old. This locomotive was another of the Western Region fleet and was allocated new to Danygraig, Swansea.
A. Sugden

The Diesel Shunter

Above: *The tramway lines around Weymouth Quay were a stronghold for the Class 03s for many years, powering both freight and boat train services through the streets of the town. No D2180 is seen on 7 July 1971 arriving at Weymouth Quay station with the 09.35 boat train from Waterloo.* John Scrace

Below: *Clearances through the streets of Weymouth were a major problem, with cars and trailers frequently blocking the railway right of way. On 16 July 1972, No D2197 slowly traverses the tramway with the down boat train from Waterloo.* J. Price

Above: *Dual brake-fitted No D2398, complete with bell on the cab end, traverses the Weymouth tramway line in December 1970 with a freight train from Eastleigh.* B. L. Jackson

Left: *A batch of Class 03s which were used on the Southern Region were modified with air brakes in the late 1960s and fitted with high-level connections to enable coupling to SR EMU and DMU stock. Additionally, locomotives allocated to work over the unprotected Weymouth Tramway line were fitted with a flashing light and warning bell, which plugged into the locomotive when needed. These fittings are seen on No D2180 at Weymouth Quay on 7 July 1971.*
John Scrace

Below: *If double heading of trip workings was required to be operated by pairs of standard small 0-6-0s, the locomotives would usually be coupled cab to cab, as demonstrated here by Nos D2074 and D2071 traversing the Silksworth Colliery branch at Ryhope on 24 August 1967.*
E. Knight

Left: Six of the Landore, Swansea, allocation of Class 03s were modified with reduced cab height to allow operation over the restricted clearances of the Burry Port & Gwendraeth Valley line in West Wales. The locomotives also received early-design headlights, clipped on the lamp irons, together with a unique multiple operating system allowing two locomotives to be coupled cab to cab for operation by one crew. Vacuum brake-fitted cut-down cab Nos 03145 and 03141 are seen at Cardiff Canton on 6 July 1985. No 03145 also appears to have its middle marker light removed.
Colin J. Marsden

Right: *Although allocated to Landore depot in Swansea, the BPGV locomotives were usually to be found at Llanelli when not in use. On 8 May 1982, full BR rail blue-liveried No 03151 is seen on shed at Llanelli with other Class 03s and a Class 37. The best way to identify a 'cut-down' Class 03 is by the reduced height of the forward facing cab windows.*
Colin J. Marsden

Left: *Looking in a rather decrepit condition, No 03120 is seen coupled back to back with No 03144 at Llanelli on 17 May 1985. The cable connections between the two locomotives to enable multiple operation are seen towards the middle of the cab end. No 03120 was introduced in October 1959 and remained working in West Wales for its entire life. It was withdrawn in February 1986 and is now preserved by Bill McAlpine at Fawley Hill Railway, Buckinghamshire.*
Colin J. Marsden

The Diesel Shunter

Above: *Working triple-headed in less than ideal conditions, Nos 03119/42/20 plunge through flood water with a full load of coal on the BPGV line just west of Pembrey on 13 February 1981. After the Class 03s were displaced from this route, BR converted a batch of Class 08s with cut down cabs.*
B. Masters

Below: *A pair of cut-down cab Class 03s, Nos 03145 and 03141 await their next turn of duty at Burry Port Yard on 12 September 1979, while on the right sister locomotive No 03119 stands coupled to a brake van.*
Brian Morrison

The Diesel Shunter

This page: *For many years Doncaster was the only BR Workshop facility to undertake the classified overhaul of the Class 03 fleet. However heavy overhauls were also undertaken by the regional maintenance facilities around the country. In the upper view, three class members Nos 03107, 03067 and 03168 await attention in a siding adjacent to the Crimpsall factory. The picture below, which looks very much like a kit of parts, shows No 03045 awaiting attention at Doncaster in June 1979.*
Derek Porter/Colin J. Marsden

The Diesel Shunter

Above: *The addition of air brake equipment to the Class 03s, saw the mounting of a large air reservoir on the running plate just in front of the cab on both sides. Buffer beam additions consisted of two main reservoir pipes and one brake pipe, with some locomotives, as shown on No D2398, having duplicate high-level connections. No D2398 is seen traversing the Weymouth Tramway on 7 July 1971 powering the 15.50 Weymouth Quay-Waterloo. The Class 03 would have worked as far as Weymouth Town station from where a Class 33 would have taken over to London.*
John Scrace.

Right: *Another of the dual brake fitted locomotives with high level connections is No 03197 seen at Yarmouth Vauxhall on 28 August 1979 shunting stock off a West Sussex Railway Touring Trust (WSRTT) charter.*
Colin J. Marsden

The Diesel Shunter

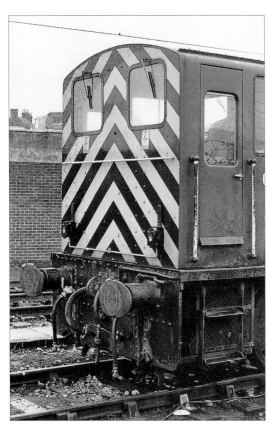

Above: *Numerically the last locomotive of the build, No 03399, introduced in October 1961 and fitted with dual brake equipment is seen at Doncaster Works in company with No 03073 on 31 August 1982.*
Colin J. Marsden

Left: *Cab end detail of dual brake fitted No 03059. This locomotive is not fitted with high-level duplicate connections.*
Colin J. Marsden

Above: *Station pilot work was undertaken at Newcastle by Class 03s right up until the mid-1980s, with usually two locomotives to be found in the station area, each coupled to a shunting match truck. No 03022 is seen stabled in the middle road at Newcastle Central on 20 May 1982 with a dual-brake 'runner' on the front.*
Colin J. Marsden

Left: *Looking rather the worse for wear after being used through the acid cleaning coach wash, No 03063 is seen inside Doncaster Works on 21 August 1981 while receiving a classified overhaul.*
Colin J. Marsden

Right: *The Newcastle station pilot work was performed by a handful of locomotives based at Newcastle Gateshead depot. To enable more modern stock to be shunted, these duties were required to be covered by a dual-brake fitted locomotive. No 03112 is seen in the south bay of the station on 28 June 1983.*
Colin J. Marsden

The Diesel Shunter

Left: *The area around Birkenhead was another which retained Class 03 operation quite late on through the 1980s, operating on some of the lines with restricted clearances. On 10 October 1983, BR rail blue-liveried No 03170 is seen with a short 'trip' scrap working near Birkenhead. This locomotive remained in operation until March 1989 and is now preserved at Barrow Hill.* Colin J. Marsden

Right: *The area around Ipswich was another which retained Class 03 operation through to the 1980s. The last locomotive of the build, No 03399 (the original D2399), is seen stabled in a siding adjacent to Ipswich station, coupled to a match truck on 27 September 1980. In the early 1980s, this locomotive gained a yellow flashing roof light for operation in Ipswich docks.* Colin J. Marsden

Left: *At first glance it looks as if this locomotive is painted in an off-white livery. It is in fact painted in standard BR rail blue, but has faded through constant passing through the acid coach wash at Botanic Gardens depot in Hull. The locomotive is seen 'on shed' with a match wagon in June 1980. On the left is a Trans-Pennine Class 124 unit.* Colin J. Marsden

The Diesel Shunter

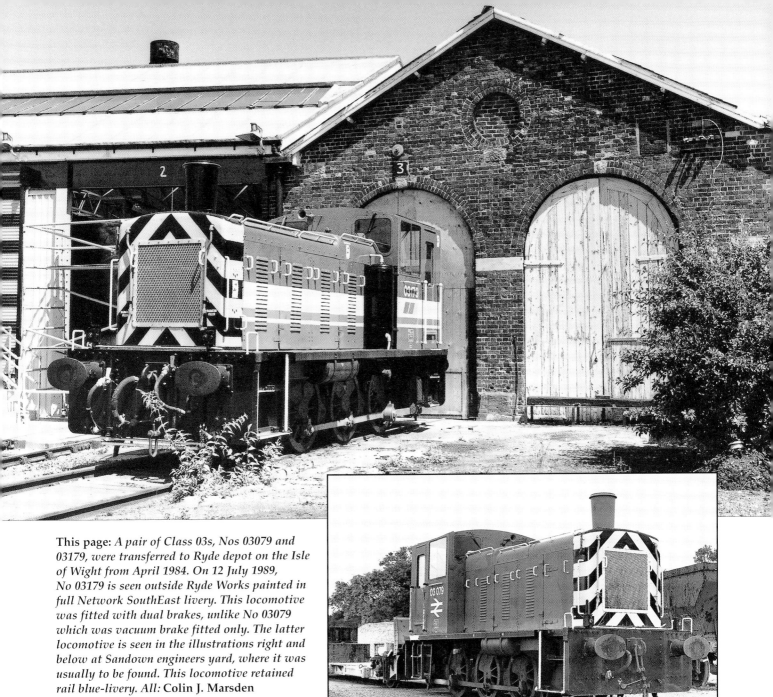

This page: *A pair of Class 03s, Nos 03079 and 03179, were transferred to Ryde depot on the Isle of Wight from April 1984. On 12 July 1989, No 03179 is seen outside Ryde Works painted in full Network SouthEast livery. This locomotive was fitted with dual brakes, unlike No 03079 which was vacuum brake fitted only. The latter locomotive is seen in the illustrations right and below at Sandown engineers yard, where it was usually to be found. This locomotive retained rail blue-livery.* All: **Colin J. Marsden**

Above: *A number of Class 03s were taken into industrial service when withdrawn from revenue service with BR. No D2181 was one such example. Withdrawn on 11 May 1968 it entered industrial service firstly with A. R. Adams and then the NCB in South Wales. On 8 October 1985 the loco, now named* **Pride of Gwent,** *is seen shunting at Gwent Coal Depot, Newport.*
Stephen Bell

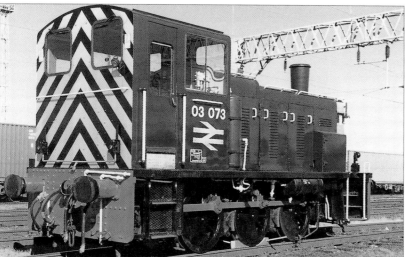

Middle Left: *The preservation movement has claimed a number of Class 03s, with many light railways finding the machines very useful for casual operations. No 03073 was withdrawn from Birkenhead in May 1989 and is now preserved at the Railway Age, Crewe, where it has been restored into full 1973-style BR rail blue.*
Darren Ford

Below Left: *During its last few years of working from Birkenhead depot, Class 03 No 03162 was returned to BR green livery, adorned with its original number and given the painted name* **Birkenhead South 1879- 1985.** *After withdrawal the locomotive entered preservation and is currently to be found on the Llangollen Railway, where this illustration was taken on 13 March 1994.*
Chris Dixon

The Diesel Shunter

Above: *The Paignton & Dartmouth Railway own and operate one ex-BR Class 03, No D2192. This locomotive was withdrawn by BR on 25 January 1969 and sold to the Dart Valley Railway Association. It is now restored to BR green livery, complete with yellow and black wasp ends and apart from depot pilot work at Paignton and Churston, takes part in diesel gala events held on the line. The locomotive is seen with a demonstration freight to the west of Churston.*
Colin J. Marsden

Below: *One of the most momentous recent events to surround the Class 03 fleet has been the repainting of former Isle of Wight-based No 03179 into West Anglia Great Northern livery for use as pilot at Hornsey depot in North London. The locomotive is seen 'on shed' at Hornsey on 25 September 1998, the day it was unveiled in this rather gaudy livery.*
Darren Ford

Drewry Car Co, Vulcan Foundry, RSH Newcastle & Darlington 0-6-0 diesel-mechanical 11100-15/21-35/49-60, 11212-11229 D2200-D2341 Class 04

The roots of this fleet can be traced back to 1947, when The Drewry Car Co built a demonstrator 0-6-0 diesel-mechanical locomotive for trial on the LNER, working in Gorton and East Anglia. The little machine, painted appropriately in LNER light green livery, worked successfully. However, with the LNER about to be absorbed into the nationalised rail network, nothing came of any subsequent orders. This 0-6-0 locomotive was announced by Drewry as a refinement of the 0-4-0 locomotive No 7050 built for the LMS in 1934.

Following Nationalisation, the Chief Mechanical Engineer of the day, R. A. Riddles, established his policy of replacing steam power for shunting as soon as possible. A problem arose in areas of restricted clearance, such as dock or tramway lines, where the larger 0-6-0 locomotives could not operate. With this in mind a fleet of 0-6-0 Drewry diesel-mechanical shunters was ordered in 1952, assembly being effected by Drewry and Vulcan Foundry in Newton-le-Willows. Subsequent orders were placed and eventually a production run of 142 locomotives was made (140 new locos, plus a 1956-built loan locomotives, which eventually became D2340 and the 1947 demonstrator, which became departmental No DS1173, eventually No D2341). Later-built locomotives were assembled at the Robert Stephenson & Hawthorns factories in Newcastle and Darlington.

The first loco, carrying the 1957-series number 11100, emerged in May 1952 and was allocated to the former LNER Wisbech & Uphill Tramway; subsequent locomotives also went to the tramway system as well as Ipswich Docks. These early locomotives of the fleet (11100-3) were supplied with full running gear protection for working over street sections and were also fitted with 'cow catchers'. Follow-on orders were soon placed and by spring 1953 new deliveries were being made, initially going to the North Eastern operating area. The first four 'dock' locomotives were structurally different from the later production run, in having only one small cab-side window, whereas later locomotives had a two-piece window opening.

Locomotives up to No 11219 were delivered to former LNER sheds, the next batch up to No 11229 went new to the Southern Region. After this the five-digit 1948 numbering system was replaced by the 1957-series with locomotives from D2260 going to the North Eastern, Eastern and Southern Regions. The final locomotive of the new build, No D2339, emerged in October 1961.

Several structural changes were made to this fleet during construction, mainly involving the exhaust stacks. Initially no exhaust pipe was fitted, with emissions being expelled through a hole in the roof of the nose end of the locomotive. Blow down problems onto the cab dictated that a simple exhaust stack was installed to lift the emissions to above cab height, this consisting of a piece of straight pipe! Later locomotives were fitted with conical or 'Saxa' shape stacks.

To improve operating performance and to give clearance for running over third rail fitted areas in the Southern Region, the size of the driving wheels was progressively enlarged from 3ft 3in to 3ft 6in and eventually to 3ft 7in.

The livery applied to locomotives when constructed was standard BR black, offset by the 1950s Lion over Wheel logo on the cab side. Locomotives built after D2260 emerged in Brunswick or locomotive green livery, complete with the Lion over Crown British Railways cab side logo. Yellow/black wasp ends were progressively applied to all locos. A handful of locomotives retained and overhauled post 1967 were repainted in corporate rail blue with yellow/black wasp warning ends.

In the late-1960s numeric classification system, this batch was given the identity of Class 04, but no locomotives remained in traffic late enough to carry the 04-prefixed number.

Initially train braking was not installed, though some locomotives had equipment fitted, but sealed off. Locomotive braking was by straight air brake equipment. Later builds were fitted with vacuum train brakes. Electric marker lights were fitted from new.

Left: *In original as delivered condition, No 11103 in black livery with Lion over Wheel logo is seen at March depot on 29 June 1952, just after delivery from Vulcan Foundry.* **Author's collection**

Right: *Devoid of its 'cow catcher' and motion protection plates, the pioneer member of the fleet No 11100 is seen looking rather the worse for wear at Stratford depot on 7 July 1959.* **R. K. Evans**

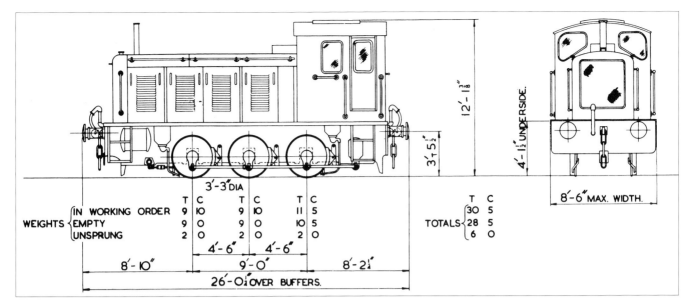

WEIGHTS	IN WORKING ORDER	T 9	C 10	T 9	C 10	T 11	C 5
	EMPTY	9	0	9	0	10	5
	UNSPRUNG	2	0	2	0	2	0

3'-3" DIA

TOTALS T 30 C 5 / 28 5 / 6 0

12'-1⅛"

3'-5½"

4'-1½" UNDERSIDE.

8'-6" MAX. WIDTH.

8'-10"   9'-0"   8'-2¼"

4'-6"   4'-6"

26'-0¼" OVER BUFFERS.

1948 number range:	11100-11229
1957 number range:	D2200-D2341 Note 1
Former class codes:	DMS1
	D2200-D2214 - DJ12/1, later D2/3
	D2215-D2340 - DJ12/2, later D2/13
Built by:	Drewry Car Co, Vulcan Foundry & RSH Newcastle & Darlington
Years introduced:	1952-1961
Wheel arrangement:	0-6-0
Weight:	30.5 tonnes
Height:	12ft 1³/₈in
Length:	26ft 0in
Width:	8ft 6in
Wheelbase:	9ft 0in
Wheel diameter:	D2200-D2214 - 3ft 3in
	D2215-D2340 - 3ft 6in
Min curve negotiable:	2 chains
Engine type:	Gardner 8L3
Engine output:	204hp
Power at rail:	152hp
Tractive effort:	D2200-D2214 - 16,850lb
	D2215-D2340 - 15,650lb

Cylinder bore:	5¹/₂in
Cylinder stroke:	7³/₄in
Maximum speed:	D2200-D2214 - 25mph
	D2215-D2340 - 27mph
Brake type:	Air on loco, vacuum on train
Brake force:	14 tons
Route availability:	1
Heating type:	Not fitted
Multiple coupling type:	Not fitted
Transmission:	Mechanical
	Engine-gearbox — Vulcan Sinclair 23
	Gearbox — Wilson Drewry CAJ-R7
	Final drive — Drewry
Gear ratio:	§
Fuel tank capacity:	225-300gal
Cooling water capacity:	40gal
Lub oil capacity:	8gal
Sanding equipment:	Pneumatic

Note
1: No D2341 added to stock in 1967 from departmental fleet as DS1173, introduced in July 1947

Above: *These small 0-6-0 mechanical shunters were initially built for use over tramway or dock lines, hence the fitting of 'cow catchers' and motion protectors. Here we see No 11101 running through the streets at Yarmouth Docks on 15 July 1952, just eight weeks after delivery.*
B. Lockey

Right: *A true period piece of diesel shunter history. Taken at Wisbech East on 9 June 1953, No 11102 makes ready to depart over the tramway line with a brake van. On the far left is sister No 11103 awaiting to perform shunting duties.*
R. E. Vincent

Below: *One of the follow-on orders for Drewry 0-6-0 shunters, No 11217, commissioned on 14 December 1956 at Percy Main shed, is seen posed for its official portrait picture at the builders works, complete with an engineer standing by the cab side for scale.*
Author's collection

Below Right: *Painted in black livery with a red buffer beam, No 11226 is seen at Hither Green, leading an engineers train in the track assembly sidings in June 1958. Note in the foreground two electrified tracks of the Lee spur line linking the Dartford Loop route with the main line. This locomotive remained working on the Southern Region for its entire life until withdrawn in 1968.*
Author's collection

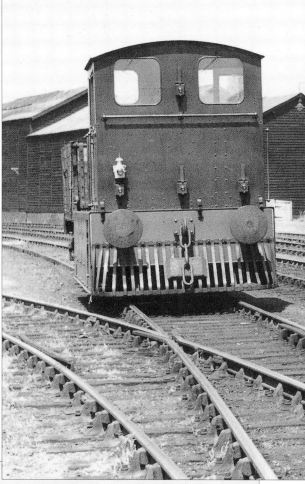

The Diesel Shunter

The Diesel Shunter

Left: *After delivery of the first few Drewry 0-6-0s, which had either no exhaust stack or just a narrow tube to lift exhaust, all production locomotives were fitted with a 'Saxa' style exhaust stack. Most locomotives were also fitted with vacuum train brake equipment from new. No 11224, delivered on 26 April 1957 to Hither Green, is seen awaiting its next duty at Eastleigh on 7 October 1961. Above the radiator grille on the front end can be seen a steam style '71A' shed plate, indicating that at this time the locomotive was based at Eastleigh.*
R. H. Wells

Right: *Compared to the previous illustration, this view of No 11123 at Stratford on 22 July 1955 shows a different style of buffer, with flat tops and base. A step is also provided on the front end to the right, while only four front lights are provided. No 11123 was delivered to Stratford on 28 July 1955 and remained on the Eastern Region until withdrawn in 1972.*
G. Wheeler

Left: *One of the last locomotives to be delivered carrying a 1948 series running number, No 11222 was one of the Southern Region fleet, built by RSH and fitted with slightly larger driving wheels to assist in clearance of the connecting rods over the third rail. In pristine condition, No 11222 is seen in black livery at Brighton in April 1957, just days after delivery. This locomotive, renumbered to D2252 in January 1962, remained at various SR sheds until withdrawn in October 1968.*
W. S. Sellar

The Diesel Shunter

This page: *Locomotives delivered from December 1957 carried the BR 1957 'D 'prefix numbers from new. In these two illustrations No. D2264, introduced to Bradford Hammerton Street on 28 December 1957 is seen at its home shed on 8 January the following year, prior to being given its first shunting work. The locomotive remained at Bradford for 10 years before being re-allocated to Leeds in 1967 and being withdrawn in 1969. Locomotives delivered after No D2260 emerged from new in BR locomotive green livery. In the illustration below, the 0-6-0 diesel mechanical shares depot accommodation with English Electric Type 1 No D8010, another virtually new locomotive at the time, having been delivered in October 1957 to the London Midland Region. Both:* **Gavin Morrison**

The Diesel Shunter

Left: *By the look of the re-decoration on the cab side, No D2248 had only just been renumbered from 11218 in this March 1959 illustration of the locomotive on shed at North Blyth. After the 1957 renumbering was authorised 'kits' of transfer numbers and revised BR logos were shipped to depots for application. However in the main this work was done at the next major overhaul or repaint.*
P. J. Sharpe

Middle Left: *Still with its 'cow catchers' fitted, but the side protection removed, No D2210 (note the small size 'D') stands at Norwich Thorpe in April 1961. This locomotive was delivered in September 1954 and was originally numbered 11111, being given its 1957-series identity on 14 June 1958.*
John C. Baker

Below: *By the time this illustration was taken in May 1963, No 11101 had been renumbered to D2201 and it was painted in BR standard locomotive green livery complete with yellow and black wasp ends. However the original 'scaffold pole' exhaust stack remained. The locomotive is seen with a short train of five vehicles at Upwell, forming the morning freight from Wisbech.*
E. Gadsden

The Diesel Shunter

This page: *Two superb views of shunting operations in progress at Yarmouth Vauxhall in August 1960. The locomotive is tramway-modified No D2212 (the original 11113). These views clearly show how the side protectors became rather dented and worn with use. These side panels were hinged at the top, to allow them to be lifted for the driver to keep the motion oiled. It is interesting to note that even the section behind the footsteps was sheeted in.*
Both: John C. Baker

Above: *The Southern Region allocation of Drewry 0-6-0s were frequently used for trip freight workings. Here we see No D2288, introduced in April 1960, painted in BR locomotive green, passing Wimbledon West with a trip freight working from Raynes Park Goods. On the up local line is a 4SUB unit forming a Shepperton-Waterloo service.* John Faulkner

Centre left: *An excellent view to show the cab end layout. No D2295 is seen hauling a 'Channel Island Boat Express' through the streets of Weymouth on 17 July 1964. These Drewry locomotives were used over the Weymouth Quay tramway line before the Class 03s were introduced in the area.* C. Symes

Left: *Obviously taken after the introduction of standard BR data panels (cab side, to right of logo), No D2216 is seen at Stratford in January 1969 while officially in store. This locomotive was then sold to P. Wood of Queenborough, Kent and exported to Italy and was last reported stored but operational at ISA, Ospitaletto.* Colin J. Marsden

The Diesel Shunter

Above: *The final working of the Upwell-Wisbech tramway section was on 20 May 1966, when No D2201 operated the service. It is seen here passing Outwell church and passing the route into railway history.*
L. Sandler

Right: *A number of Drewry 0-6-0s, later classified as 04 under the BR TOPS system, found their way into industrial use. One such locomotive was No D2310 which for many years worked in the coal sidings at Tolworth in South London, operated by Colmec. After its useful life was over here, No D2310 entered preservation and is now at the Battlefield Railway.*
Colin J. Marsden

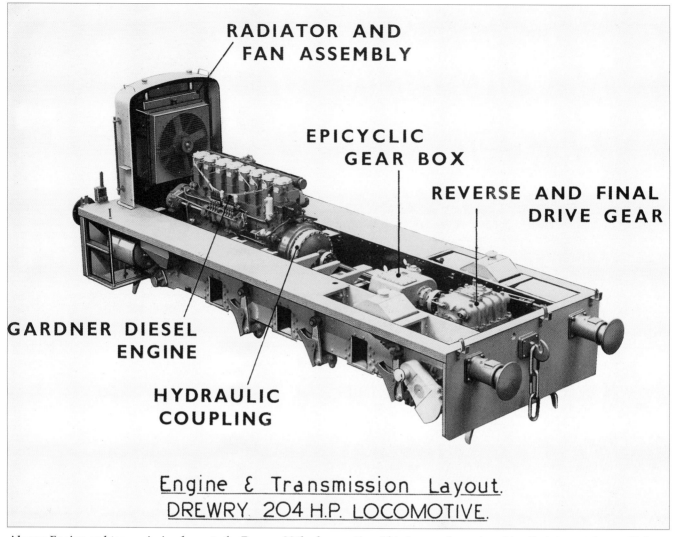

RADIATOR AND
FAN ASSEMBLY

EPICYCLIC
GEAR BOX

REVERSE AND FINAL
DRIVE GEAR

GARDNER DIESEL
ENGINE

HYDRAULIC
COUPLING

Engine & Transmission Layout.
DREWRY 204 H.P. LOCOMOTIVE.

Above: Engine and transmission layout of a Drewry 204hp locomotive. This is one of a series of 'real' pictures taken at Vulcan Foundry during assembly of the first batch of locomotives in order to provide illustrations for the training manual.
Ian Allan Library

Below: A very rare illustration of the original Drewry 204hp demonstrator, which later became No DS1173. At the time of this illustration, the locomotive was still in the ownership of Drewry Car and was about to go 'on loan' to the LNER.
Author's collection

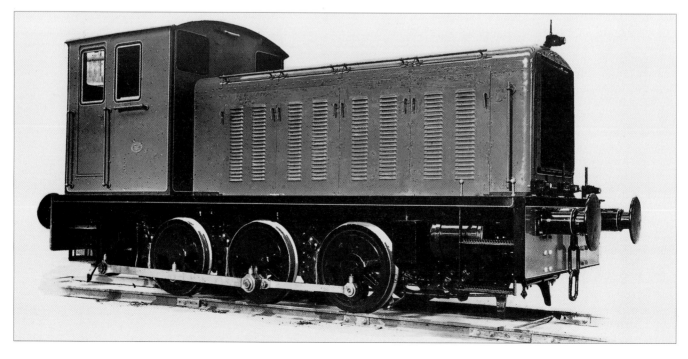

Above: *After its departmental career was over, No DS1173 was allocated to the revenue fleet. It took the next available slot in the Drewry 0-6-0 fleet in 1967 and was thus numbered D2341. The locomotive is seen on shed at Hither Green, alongside 'Crompton' No D6572 on 14 January 1968.* **David Percival**

Below: *Painted in a non-standard mid-blue livery, No D2271 is now preserved in full working order on the West Somerset Railway. It is seen here at the head of two milk tanks and a brake van at Minehead in June 2000.* **Colin J. Marsden**

The Diesel Shunter

Andrew Barclay 0-6-0 diesel-mechanical
11177-11186
D2400-D2409

Among the mass orders given to different suppliers to build small diesel shunters as part of the modernisation project, was this batch of 10 from Andrew Barclay of Kilmarnock. The locomotives, based on the builder's industrial design, were fitted with the trusted Gardner 8L3 power unit developing 204hp at 1,200rpm. Traction was via a Wiseman 4-speed SE4 gearbox.

The batch was all destined for the Eastern Region and was delivered between July 1956 and March 1957 to Kings Cross and Lincoln depots, eventually being concented in the Lincolnshire area.

The exterior design of this fleet was very much from the industrial stable, being a larger version of the D2953 (11503) series (see p.136). To say its appearance was basic was an under statement and it appears that at the time Andrew Barclay did not have much of an aesthetic eye for design.

The fleet, while returning a good miles/hours per casualty figure, was deemed as non-standard under the National Traction Plan and was thus phased out of service in the 1967-69 period, much of their shunting role being dispensed with by more modern methods of freight operation and the general decline in wagon load freight services. All ten locomotives were sold for scrap, none entering the private or industrial world.

When built the fleet was released to traffic in standard BR black, complete with a Lion over Wheel logo on the cab side, most examples later being repainted into standard locomotive green.

Electric front and rear end markers were fitted from new. One major problem with this Andrew Barclay design was the angled fuel tank mounted on top of the main engine compartment structure just ahead of the cab which drastically restricted the drivers forward vision when compared with the similar-output BR design small 204hp locos.

Left: The first of the Andrew Barclay 0-6-0 diesel-mechanical build, No 11177 is seen at Hatfield on 4 August 1956, just two weeks after delivery. The first two locomotives of the build were allocated new to King's Cross for just two months, before going with the rest of the fleet to Lincoln. A. W. Martin

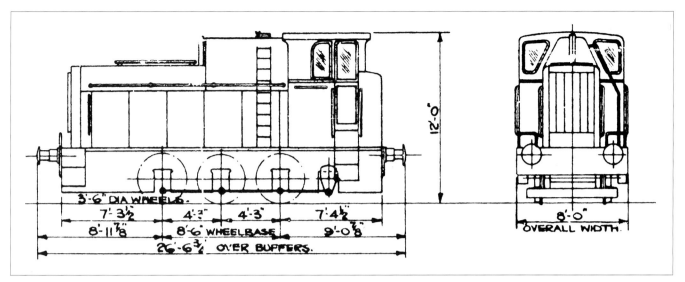

BR 1948 number range:	11177-11186	Tractive effort:	15,350lb
BR 1957 number range:	D2400-D2409	Cylinder bore:	5^{1}/$_{2}$in
Former class code:	DJ14, later D2/5, 2/12	Cylinder stroke:	7^{3}/$_{4}$in
Built by:	Andrew Barclay	Maximum speed:	17^{3}/$_{4}$mph
Years introduced:	1956-1957	Brake type:	Air on loco, no train brakes
Wheel arrangement:	0-6-0	Brake force:	15 tons
Weight:	32 tons	Route availability:	1
Height:	12ft 0in	Heating type:	Not fitted
Length:	26ft 6^{3}/$_{4}$in	Multiple coupling type:	Not fitted
Width:	8ft 0in	Transmission type:	Mechanical
Wheelbase:	8ft 6in		Engine-gearbox — Vulcan
Wheel diameter:	3ft 6in		Gearbox — Wilson Drewry CA5
Min curve negotiable:	2 chains	Fuel tank capacity:	400gal
Engine type:	Gardner 8L3	Cooling water capacity:	115
Engine output:	204hp	Lub oil capacity:	35
Power at rail:	122hp	Sanding equipment:	Pneumatic

Left: *The first of the ten Andrew Barclay 204hp diesel-mechanical shunters emerged from the Kilmarnock factory in late June 1956 and took up trials in the local area before being transferred south. This posed illustration shows an immaculate No 11177, painted in BR standard locomotive black livery, with Lion over Wheel logo on the cab side. A classic Andrew Barclay oval makers plate was positioned between the logo and number.* **Author's collection**

Left: *It could never be said that these Andrew Barclay locomotives looked very pretty, but they were rugged workhorses and by the accounts of driving staff operated well. No 11186 is seen at Boston. This was the last locomotive of the build and emerged from Kilmarnock on 1 March 1957. It was renumbered to D2409 in January 1961 and withdrawn on 28 December 1968.*
T. Booth

Right: *In the days before yellow vests had to be worn when on or about the track, two shunting staff sort out operations at King's Lynn in April 1961 using No 11183. The shunter on the cab steps of the locomotive is holding a shunting pole, used to unhook the link couplings between wagons without the need to physically go between vehicles.*
John C. Baker

Left: *Although only 22 months old when this picture was taken at Immingham, No 11177 looks rather more decrepit than in the illustration on the previous page when it posed for the official construction view. One interesting point on this design and many other early diesel shunters was the use of a wooden cab door.*
P. Norton

The Diesel Shunter

Above: *Towards the end of its operating life in 1967, the pioneer locomotive of the fleet, which had become No D2400 in November 1960, is seen 'on shed' at Barrow Hill.*
Author's collection

Left: *With its connecting rod from the drive to the centre wheelset laying on the running plate, No D2409 is seen in transit at Doncaster in June 1961.*
A. Bunch

Below: *Apparently in BR locomotive green livery, sporting the BR Lion over Crown logo and yellow/black wasp ends, No D2403 is seen at Immingham in March 1964.*
A. Hardy

The Diesel Shunter

Andrew Barclay 0-4-0 diesel-mechanical
D2410-D2444
Class 06
06001-06010

Under the modernisation plan, the Scottish Region had a need for powerful short wheelbase 0-4-0 diesel-mechanical shunting power which had to be suitable for both shunting and trip freight operations. The answer to this need came in this fleet of just 7ft wheelbase machines built by Andrew Barclay of Kilmarnock, powered by the same Gardner 204hp prime mover as used in the company's 0-6-0 locomotives.

A total of 35 locomotives were ordered in two batches, which were all delivered to the Scottish Region between June 1958 and October 1960, the allocation being split between the principal regional depots. As the fleet was identified for trip workings, vacuum train braking was fitted from new, locomotive braking being achieved by straight air brakes.

The structural design of this fleet, classified D2/6 under the original BR system, was very similar to the 0-4-0 and 0-6-0 industrial units of the day, but did have a slightly more pleasing cab design. However, the forward vision, as on the larger 0-6-0 series, was largely obstructed by the fuel tank, mounted ahead of the cab above the engine compartment.

One noticeable structural change was made during the build. On locomotives Nos D2410-D2424 three rear cab windows were provided, whereas those numbered above D2425 had only two windows.

This is another of the classes which were delivered into a very uncertain world in terms of deployment. The National Traction Plan called for a reduction in fleet size and some withdrawals were made in 1967. However some examples remained working north of the Border until 1981 when the survivors were withdrawn from revenue earning service. By that time however, departmental service called for one example which was transferred to Reading Signal Works as No 97804.

As this class remained in service after the early 1970s, TOPS numeric classification 06 was given to the fleet, with surviving members renumbered into the five-digit 06 prefixed number from 1973.

When built, the fleet was finished in BR locomotive green, without yellow/black warning ends, but with red buffer beam. The second design of motif, Lion over Crown, was applied to the bodyside. Repaints from the late 1960s were in BR corporate rail blue with yellow/black wasp ends, offset by yellow buffer beams and a white BR double arrow logo on the power unit side panelling. Nose and cab-end electric marker lights were fitted from new.

Below: Thankfully Andrew Barclay always took record illustrations of the first locomotive of each order. This illustration reveals that for some reason totally non-standard running numbers were applied to the first of the 0-4-0 build, which eventually became BR Class 06. No D2410 was released from the AB factory in Kilmarnock on 12 June 1958 and shedded at Inverness from 19 June. Author's collection

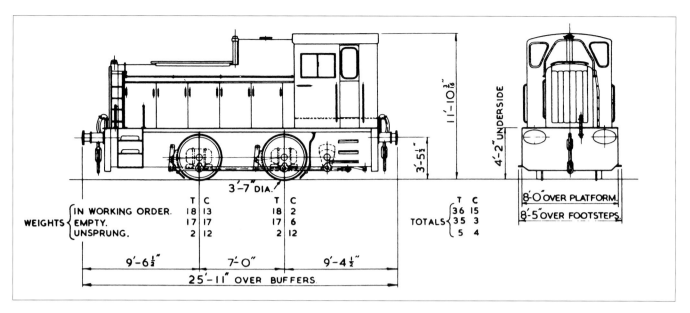

TOPS numbers:	06001-06010		Cylinder bore:	5¹/₂in
1957 BR number range:	D2410-D2444		Cylinder stroke:	7³/₄in
Former class codes:	D2/6, later 2/12		Maximum speed:	22³/₄mph
Built by:	Andrew Barclay		Brake type:	Air on loco, vacuum on train
Years introduced:	1958-1960		Brake force:	15 tons
Wheel arrangement:	0-4-0		Route availability:	5
Weight:	37 tons		Heating type:	Not fitted
Height:	11ft 10¹/₄in		Multiple coupling type:	Not fitted
Length:	25ft 11in		Transmission:	Mechanical
Width:	8ft 5in			Engine-gearbox — Vulcan Type 23
Wheelbase:	7ft 0in			Gearbox — Wilson Drewry CA5
Wheel diameter:	3ft 7in			Final drive — Wiseman 15RLGB
Min curve negotiable:	2 chains		Gear ratio:	§
Engine type:	Gardner 8L3		Fuel tank capacity:	325gal
Engine output:	204hp		Cooling water capacity:	50gal
Power at rail:	152hp		Lub oil capacity:	8gal
Tractive effort:	19,800lb		Sanding equipment:	Pneumatic

Right: *By the time the fourth locomotive of the build emerged, No D2413 in early October 1958, standard identity transfers had been obtained, that is perhaps why a second official record view of the class was taken. Painted in BR standard locomotive green from introduction, this locomotive went to Inverness shed where it remained until 1966 when it was transferred to Dunfermline. This locomotive eventually became TOPS No 06001.*
Author's collection

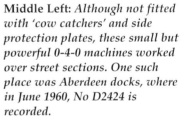

Above: *Many, if not all, the designs of Andrew Barclay shunters were offered as 'off-the-shelf' industrial units, with differing body shells to suit the customer. Here we see an industrial 0-4-0 diesel hydraulic unit built for the CEGB at High Marnham Power Station, buffered up to 0-4-0 BR unit No D2424, which emerged from Kilmarnock in April 1959.*
Author's collection

Middle Left: *Although not fitted with 'cow catchers' and side protection plates, these small but powerful 0-4-0 machines worked over street sections. One such place was Aberdeen docks, where in June 1960, No D2424 is recorded.*
E. Craig

Below Left: *Access to the power unit and transmission equipment was achieved by five removable doors on each side of the body. These were unlocked by the two twist handles at the top, which allowed the door to drop forward and then be removed. No D2412 is seen at Eastfield on 28 September 1958, while on delivery from Kilmarnock to Inverness.*
I. Smith

The Diesel Shunter

Above: *Major inroads were made into this fleet in the late 1960s with over half the fleet being withdrawn as surplus to requirements. The remaining locomotives were eventually renumbered under TOPS to Class 06. No 06002, the original No D2414 is seen inside Dunfermline Townhill depot in May 1975, soon after being overhauled and renumbered. The livery is standard BR rail blue with white number and logo with a yellow buffer beam and wasp ends.*
Colin J. Marsden

Below: *One of the most unusual duties ever performed by a class member was when preserved 4-6-2 Duchess of Sutherland was transferred to Butlin's holiday camp in Ayr. No D2434 and BR standard 0-6-0 No D3005 were given the job of hauling just the locomotive over to Greenan Sidings on the Heads of Ayr branch.*
Derek Cross

This page: *With life left in several members of this fleet when withdrawn from revenue-earning service, a departmental career followed for a small number. No 06003 was renumbered to departmental 97804 and moved south to Old Oak Common and then Reading, where it was used to replace the existing 0-4-0 shunter at Reading signal works. In the above view the locomotive is seen with two service wagons at Old Oak Common, while in the view below the locomotive is seen inside the Signal & Telegraph Workshops at Reading.*
Both: Colin J. Marsden

The Diesel Shunter

Above: *Looking in a rather sorry state with a body section missing and its connecting rods removed, No 06006 in BR blue livery is seen stored at Dundee in August 1982.*
John Tuffs

Right: *After three years in Departmental use No 06003 was withdrawn and after a period in store thankfully entered preservation, firstly at Meadowhall, Sheffield and now at the Rutland Museum. No 06003 is seen restored to rail blue.*
Darren Ford

Below: *During its Departmental period at Reading, No 97804 is seen coupled to a pair of open wagons and a brakevan on Reading depot.*
Darren Ford

Hudswell Clarke 0-6-0 diesel-mechanical 11116-11120/11144-11148 D2500-D2509

Ordered by the BR in 1953, these Hudswell Clarke 0-6-0 diesel-mechanical locomotives are almost a copy of the same builder's two LMS prototype locomotives Nos 7405/6 (7055/6) built in 1934.

These 10 machines, looking very much like steam locomotives, were ordered for a specific purpose, shunting at Birkenhead Docks, where the locomotives were delivered between December 1955 and June 1956 to assist in the replacement of steam traction.

This fleet, unlike the LMS prototypes, used a Gardner 8L3 engine providing 204hp, which drove an SSS powerflow three speed forward/reverse gearbox.

Unlike any other of the 1950s jackshaft shunters, this fleet had the drive at the front end of the structure, rather than under the cab. Another distinctive feature of the design was a 'chimney' at the front end, very much like that of a steam locomotive.

The locomotives were ordered in two separate lots and onstruction was carried out at the HC factory in Leeds with Nos 11116-20 delivered in standard BR black livery, while the second batch, Nos 11144-8, emerged in BR locomotive green.

They became D2500-D2509 under the 1957 scheme, between 1958 and 1962.

Braking was only provided by a straight air system on the locomotives, no provision being made for the installation of train brakes. Weighing in at 31 tons however, the locomotives had no problem in slowing down most slow speed shunting movements.

Access to the prime mover and transmission on this design was achieved by three large hinged doors on either side of the bonnet section, while the top section of the bonnet was also removable to allow engine removal.

Visibility from the driving cab was reported to be poor, with only a very limited view of the line ahead from the cab when looking down the side of the bonnet section.

A large oval Hudswell Clarke makers plate was attached either side of the weight block at the front of the superstructure. Today these plates which carry the works numbers D898-D902 and D938-D942 are valued at several hundred pounds.

All locomotives of the design were withdrawn in 1967 under the National Traction Plan and broken up.

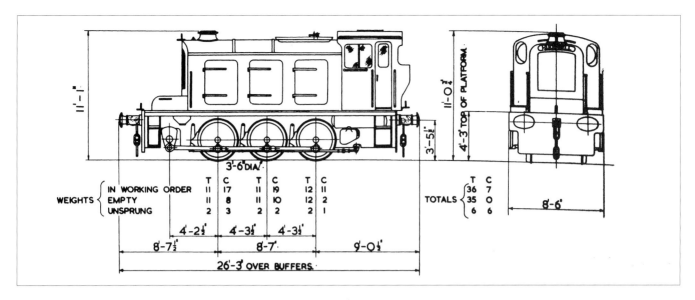

WEIGHTS		T	C	T	C	T	C	TOTALS	T	C
	IN WORKING ORDER	11	17	11	19	12	11		36	7
	EMPTY	11	8	11	10	12	2		35	0
	UNSPRUNG	2	3	2	2	2	1		6	6

BR 1948 number range:	11116-11120, 11144-11148	Tractive effort:	16,100lb
BR 1957 number range:	D2500-D2509	Cylinder bore:	5^{1}/$_{2}$in
Former class code:	D2/7, 2/14	Cylinder stroke:	7^{3}/$_{4}$in
Built by:	Hudswell Clarke	Maximum speed:	14mph
Years introduced:	1955-1956	Brake type:	Air on loco, no train brakes
Wheel arrangement:	0-6-0	Brake force:	22 tons
Weight:	36 tons	Route availability:	1
Height:	11ft 1in	Heating type:	Not fitted
Length:	25ft 11^{1}/$_{2}$in	Multiple coupling type:	Not fitted
Width:	8ft 6in	Transmission type:	Mechanical
Wheelbase:	8ft 7in		Engine-gearbox — SCR Type 23
Wheel diameter:	3ft 6in		Gearbox — SSS Power Flow
Min curve negotiable:	3 chains	Fuel tank capacity:	300gal
Engine type:	Gardner 8L3	Cooling water capacity:	125
Engine output:	204hp	Lub oil capacity:	30
Power at rail:	122hp	Sanding equipment:	Pneumatic

Below: In immaculate condition, just after delivery from the Hudswell Clarke factory, No 11118 is seen on shed at Leeds Stourton on 7 March 1956. The locomotive sports BR black livery. Note the superb cast oval makers plate towards the front end.
Author's collection

Left: Looking in many respects more like a steam locomotive than a diesel, Hudswell-Clarke No D2504 leads a line-up of the class at Birkenhead depot on 30 August 1959. These 10 locomotives were constructed for use in the massive dock complex around Liverpool and Birkenhead and were initially allocated to 6C — Birkenhead Mollington Street. This locomotive was withdrawn in March 1967 and broken up at Booth's of Rotherham.
J. Pickle

The Diesel Shunter

Left: *Still carrying its 1948 series five-digit running number, No 11146 is seen between pilot duties at Derby Works in August 1961. As can be seen access to the power unit was obtained by three body side hinged doors. At the nose or radiator end, the flat section was a weight block to improve adhesion. This locomotive was renumbered to D2507 on 28 October 1961, and remained in traffic until March 1967.* Brian Stephenson

Right: *This April 1964 view of No D2506, shows the locomotive in BR locomotive green livery, stabled at Derby Locomotive Works awaiting attention prior to returning to Barrow for shunting duties. The cast Hudswell Clarke makers plate is seen attached to the front, ahead of the radiator assembly. Behind No D2506 is LMS prototype No 10001.* John Cornelius

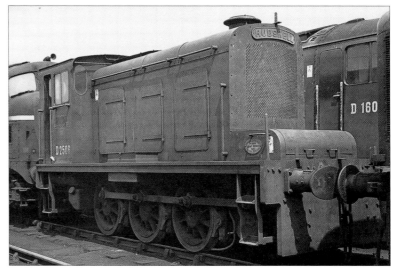

Below: *Looking more like a line up of steam locomotives than modern traction, five of the Hudswell Clarke 0-6-0 diesel-mechanical locomotives Nos D2509, D2504, D2505, D2508 and un-renumbered No 11146 stand on a smoky Birkenhead depot on 11 June 1961.* Norman Preedy

Above: *After this fleet had finished working in the dock complex around the Mersey, other uses were found before the National Traction Plan called for their withdrawal as 'non-standard' and surplus to requirements. Here No D2508 shares depot space with a Metro-Vic Co-Bo at Barrow in December 1966. This locomotive was withdrawn in May 1967 and sold to Booths of Rotherham for disposal. Note the superb cast 'Hudswell' name above the radiator, which are now collectors items.* **Author's collection**

Below: *No D2506 remained in service long enough to be painted with a yellow/black wasp warning end, as shown here on the locomotive awaiting breaking up at Steelbreaking and Dismantling Co of Chesterfield in July 1969. This locomotive was withdrawn on 25 November 1967 and moved to Derby Works as a pilot and generator.* Roger Kaye

The Diesel Shunter

Hudswell Clarke 0-6-0 diesel-mechanical D2510-D2519

Ordered by the BR in 1960 from Hudswell Clarke, as a follow-on order to the 1955-built D2500-D2509 series, these ten off-centre cab 0-6-0s with a total wheelbase of just 8ft 7in had a very short life span on the national network.

The first locomotive of the build, designated class D2/12, emerged in September 1961 and was allocated to the London Midland Region at Birkenhead depot for use in the Liverpool Dock area. The structural style was very pleasing to the eye, with long and short 'bonnet' sections, the former housing a Gardner 8L3 engine set to deliver 204hp.

The fleet was allocated to Birkenhead, Barrow-in-Furness, Watford and Crewe South.

At the time this fleet emerged, one wonders why such an order was ever placed, as by then, the standard shunter designs of large 350hp and small 204hp locomotives were well into production.

Driving controls were provided either side of the cab, which gave excellent all round visibility for pilot and shunting work.

Very similar to the earlier Hudswell Clarke fleet in technical performance, but with much improved body styling, these locomotives only lasted for just six years on BR tracks, before the entire fleet was withdrawn between May and December 1967. All were offered to the private industrial sector, with the then National Coal Board (NCB) taking the entire fleet under its remit. No D2511 is preserved on the Keighley & Worth Valley Railway.

From new the fleet carried BR standard locomotive green livery with yellow/black warning ends and the BR Lion over Crown logo on the cab sides above the running number.

Locomotive braking was provided by air while train braking used the vacuum system. Both ends of the locomotive sported electric marker lights.

An interesting fitting to these locomotives was a protective glass screen attached to the leading face of the cabside window to provide protection to the driver.

Left: *Introduced in September 1961, No D2511 was allocated new to Barrow-in-Furness depot (12E). On 22 August 1967, the locomotive is seen from its nose end inside the depot at Barrow, which by this time was identified by the code 12C.* **Dave Percival**

Below: *One of the more pleasing designs of 0-6-0 diesel-mechanical shunters were these Hudswell-Clarke locos, built as a 'follow-on' order to the previously shown fleet. No D2518, painted in BR locomotive green is seen at Willesden Junction on 30 April 1966.* **Peter Groom**

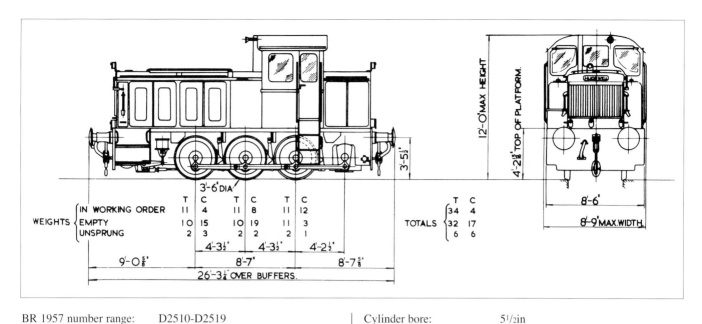

WEIGHTS		T	C		T	C		T	C
	IN WORKING ORDER	11	4		11	8		11	12
	EMPTY	10	15		10	19		11	3
	UNSPRUNG	2	3		2	2		2	1

TOTALS	T	C
	34	4
	32	17
	6	6

3'-6" DIA
4'-3½" 4'-3½" 4'-2½"
9'-0⅝" 8'-7" 8'-7⅝"
26'-3¼" OVER BUFFERS.
3'-5½"
12'-0" MAX HEIGHT
4'-2⅝" TOP OF PLATFORM.
8'-6"
8'-9" MAX. WIDTH.

BR 1957 number range:	D2510-D2519	Cylinder bore:	5½in
Former class code:	D2/12, 2/14 A	Cylinder stroke:	7¾in
Built by:	Hudswell Clarke	Maximum speed:	24mph
Year introduced:	1961	Brake type:	Air on loco, vacuum train brakes
Wheel arrangement:	0-6-0	Brake force:	13 tons
Weight:	35 tons	Route availability:	4
Height:	12ft 0in	Heating type:	Not fitted
Length:	26ft 3¼in	Multiple coupling type:	Not fitted
Width:	8ft 9in	Transmission type:	Mechanical
Wheelbase:	8ft 7in		Engine-gearbox — SCR Type 23
Wheel diameter:	3ft 6in		Gearbox — SSS Power Flow
Min curve negotiable:	3 chains		Final drive — 3-speed
Engine type:	Gardner 8L3	Fuel tank capacity:	300gal
Engine output:	204hp	Cooling water capacity:	150gal
Power at rail:	122hp	Lub oil capacity:	45gal
Tractive effort:	16,100lb	Sanding equipment:	Pneumatic

Right: *New on 2 December 1961, No D2519 was allocated to Crewe and principally used for works pilotage until withdrawn just six years later. With target number 12 on the front end, the locomotive is seen on Crewe South shed on 13 May 1964. From delivery these locomotives were fitted with vacuum train brake equipment. Although electric marker lights were also fitted, this example also sports an oil headlight. Yellow/black 'wasp' warning ends were also applied from new.*
CJM collection

The Diesel Shunter

Above: *Sharing depot space at Willesden District Electric Depot, No D2518 is viewed from its short nose end, while Class AL5 No E3050 looks on in the background.* **J. G. Turner**

Below: *D2518 was the only example of the class to be allocated to the London area, being based at Willesden (1A). It was initially delivered to Watford (1C) on 25 November 1961, transferring to Willesden in January 1963. The locomotive is seen inside Willesden roundhouse, in company with a BR Type 2 (later Class 24). It is interesting to note that the depot had applied a cast '1A' shed plate to the cab door. No D2518 was withdrawn in February 1967 and after a period in store was sold to the National Coal Board in the Doncaster area.* **G. H. Marsh**

The Diesel Shunter

Hunslet Engine Co 0-6-0 diesel-mechanical 11136-11143/11161-11176, D2550-D2618 Class 05 05001

One of the more sizeable classes of 0-6-0 diesel-mechanical shunters was this fleet of 69 units built in two lots by the Hunslet Engine Co of Leeds, following an order placed by BR in 1953.

The first locomotive of the order, carrying the number 11136, emerged in October 1955 and allocated to Ipswich. The 25ft 4in long shunter was of quite a pleasing appearance and followed a more boxey outline. Special attention was given to the design of the driving cab, to provide the operating staff with a good all-round view of operations. Driving controls were arranged on both sides of the cab. A point of design controversy was the narrow width of the cab entrance doors, which were just 15in wide!

Concurrent with the assembly of the first batch of 24 locos, came a second order taking the production run to 69. Minor structural differences were incorporated in the later batch, the most noticeable being a 12in higher cab roof, considerably improving the cab atmosphere and allowing an extra longitudinal window just below roof height. The wheel diameter was also increased by 5 inches to 3ft 9in, while the overall length of the locomotive was increased by eight inches.

On the ends of the second batch, numbered from new as D2574-D2618, emerging between July 1958 and April 1961, very deep steel buffer beams were installed fitted with oval buffers. On the original locomotives numbered below D2574 round buffers were fitted.

All locomotives were fitted with vacuum train brakes from new, together with straight air brake equipment for locomotive use. Electric marker lights were also installed from new.

The original livery was black, offset by the Lion over Wheel logo, 1960s repaints were in standard BR green, with wasp yellow/black warning ends. A notable feature was the large cast brass 'Hunslet' name on the front of the radiator housing; these were either finished with a red or yellow ground.

The majority of the fleet were withdrawn under the National Traction Plan, being deleted from stock between 1966-68. One locomotive however remained, No D2554 which was sent to the Isle of Wight in the mid 1960s as the Island's sole locomotive under modernisation. It remained in use until the 1990s when replaced by a Class 03. This sole member of the Hunslet fleet attracted the allocation of the TOPS numeric classification 05 to the design. No D2554 was later repainted into standard BR rail blue and renumbered into the TOPS system as 05001. Subsequently the locomotive was transferred to the departmental fleet as No 97803.

A small number of locomotives entered preservation or industry on withdrawal, the majority being broken up for scrap.

Below: The two breeds of Hunslet shunting power pose side by side in this illustration at Ipswich. Large Hunslet No 11136 pilots a rake of wagons through the dock line, while Baby Hunslet No 11500, complete with body protection side plates and cowcatchers looks on. Both locomotives are in as-delivered BR black livery. **CJM collection**

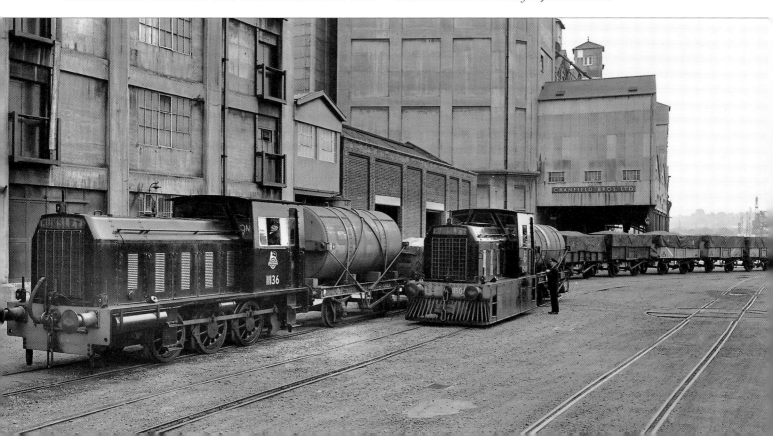

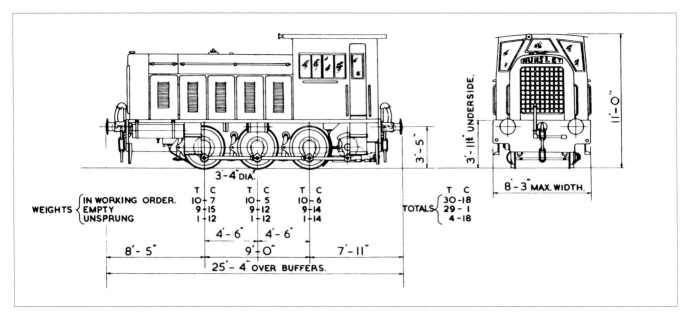

TOPS number:	05001		Power at rail:	152hp			
1948 BR number range:	11136-11143, 11161-11176		Tractive effort:	D2550-D2573 - 14,500lb			
1957 BR number range:	D2550-D2618			D2574-D2618 - 17,400lb			
Former class codes:	D2550-D2573 - DJ13. later		Cylinder bore:	5½in			
	D2/8, 2/15A		Cylinder stroke:	7¾in			
	D2574-D2618 - DJ13/2, later		Maximum speed:	18.8mph			
	D2/9, 2/15		Brake type:	Air on loco, vacuum on train			
Built by:	Hunslet Engine Co		Brake force:	21 tons			
Years introduced:	1955-1961		Route availability:	2			
Wheel arrangement:	0-6-0		Heating type:	Not fitted			
Weight:	D2550-D2573 - 31 tons		Multiple coupling type:	Not fitted			
	D2574-D2618 - 32 tons		Transmission:	Mechanical			
Height:	11ft 0in			Engine-gearbox — Hunslet			
Length:	25ft 4in			Gearbox — Hunslet			
Width:	8ft 3in			Final drive — Hunslet			
Wheelbase:	9ft 0in		Gear ratio:	§			
Wheel diameter:	D2550-D2573 - 3ft 4in		Fuel tank capacity:	300gal			
	D2574-D2618 - 3ft 9in		Cooling water capacity:	50gal			
Min curve negotiable:	1.82 chains		Lub oil capacity:	8gal			
Engine type:	Gardner 8L3		Sanding equipment:	Pneumatic			
Engine output:	204hp						

Left: The fifth locomotive of the build, No 11140, delivered from the Hunslet factory in Leeds to Ipswich in May 1956, is seen 'on shed' at Ipswich on 8 May. It has just arrived from the builders and was still awaiting commissioning. It is painted in BR black livery with a red buffer beam. This locomotive was to have a charmed life, as it was later to become D2554 and was the locomotive sent to the Isle of Wight in 1966.
T. K. Widd

The Diesel Shunter

Right: Delivered as No 11141 on 5 June 1956 to Norwich shed, black-liveried No D2555 (complete with a small 'D' prefix to its number), is seen inside Stratford Works on 7 September 1958. This locomotive remained on the Eastern Region until early 1966 when it was transferred to Speke Junction for Liverpool Division use.
A. Swain

Left: In immaculate condition, and again showing a small 'D' prefix to its number, No D2556, the original 11142 is seen 'on shed' at Ipswich on 16 June 1958. This locomotive was delivered in July 1956 and renumbered to its 1957 series identity in May 1958.
P. J. Sharpe

Right: People often think road transport of locomotives is a modern phenomenon, however this illustration dated 29 April 1968, shows that road transport was used to shift damaged No D2600 from Goole following a derailment.
D. Hardy

The Diesel Shunter

Below: One of the real classic pictures of the UK diesel shunter, No 11136, the first locomotive of the build, which was later renumbered D2550, is seen hauling an unfitted rake of general merchandise wagons through Ipswich Docks on 17 October 1955. This was one of a series of illustrations taken to mark the deployment of diesel traction in the Ipswich Docks area. **CJM collection**

Above: The final 45 locomotives of the build, were constructed with a revised structural design to the cab, with a much deeper window assembly. This view from the cab end of No 11167, delivered in May 1957, clearly shown the original shallow type. With the cab door open this picture also demonstrates how narrow the cab entry was. No 11167 is seen at Harwich Parkeston Quay in 1957.
Norman Preedy

Below: No D2574 is one of the later built locomotives, fitted with the taller cab window layout, revised front deep buffer beam, front side step, and delivered new to BR in BR locomotive green livery with the Lion over Crown logo on the cab side. This Scottish-allocated example also has its running number applied on the red buffer beam in white. Another modification to later-built locomotives was oval buffers. No D2574 was delivered new to Stranraer depot in July 1958 and is seen here in this classic freight train view on the northside of Glasgow.
Author's collection

Right: By the scuff on the cab door it look as though the door on this example was a job to open and often kicked by drivers! No D2557 is shown in black livery at Stratford depot on 18 April 1959. At the time this locomotive was allocated to Ipswich depot.
R. J. Buckley

Below: No D2556 is shown with a small 'D' prefix to its number.
P. J. Sharpe

Below: One of the later built locos, No D2614 is illustrated at Hull Docks, in June 1961. This locomotive has its running number applied on the right side of the buffer beam, is painted in locomotive green-livery, has yellow/black wasp ends and carries the target number 30 on the front lamp iron. Compared with the earlier built locomotives of this class, the front cab windows are finished with an aluminium frame. CJM collection

The Diesel Shunter

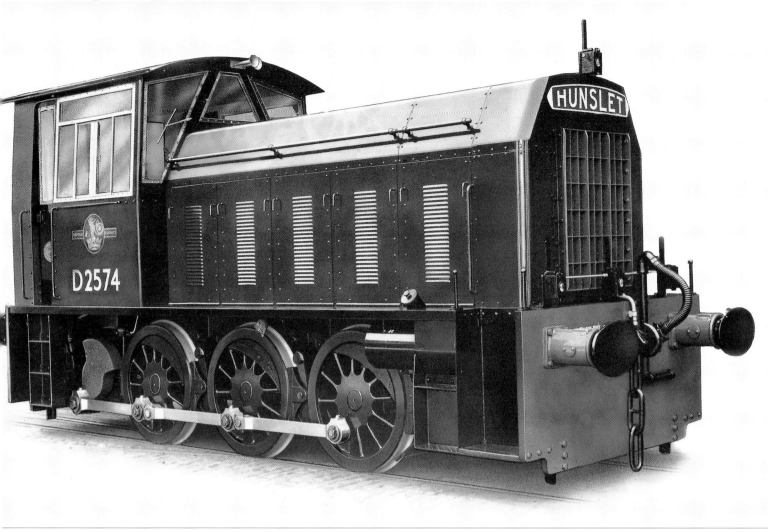

This page: *Two interesting views, showing how minor variations existed within the later designed locomotives. No D2574 above shows the Lion over Crown logo facing the front of the loco, while D2600 below has the logo facing back. The window frames of the above locomotive have square section corners, while the locomotive below has curved corners. No D2600 also has radiator filler pipes by the inner section of the buffer, a more modern design of vacuum pipe and revised radiator grilles.* **CJM collection/Peter Groom**

The Diesel Shunter

Above: When compared with illustrations of the original design locomotives of this class, a number of changes were carried out to the cab ends on later built examples. The most noticeable change was the much deeper windows to address a visibility problem. On a coal trip working from Knottingley depot, No D2617 approaches Knottingley station on 20 September 1965.
A. Swain

Below: Probably the most well-known member of this fleet was No D2554 which as part of the Isle of Wight electrification scheme in 1966 was shipped to the island and used as traction for engineering trains. When first delivered to Ryde, its official depot, the locomotive retained BR green livery, but a repaint in the early 1970s, saw corporate rail blue applied. Under numerical classification the locomotive became the sole member of Class 05 and in post-1973 renumbering became No 05001, Under BR's ownership policy the locomotive eventually became part of the departmental sector and was again renumbered to 97803. Carrying this number, the locomotive is seen at Sandown. **Colin J. Marsden**

The Diesel Shunter

Right: *Some of this Hunslet class have found their way into preservation. One such locomotive is No D2578, which was purchased by Bulmers of Hereford for private shunting and later went to the Bulmer Railway Centre. For some rather sad reason, this locomotive had gained a copper-capped chimney when photographed in November 1968. Other preservation additions are a narrow-banded yellow/black wasp buffer beam and a cast nameplate Cider Queen.* **John Sawtell**

Below: *The Hunslet design for the large 0-6-0, which became the BR Class 05 came direct from the builder's industrial catalogue. Here a virtually identical loco, except for revised radiator grilles, a large headlamp, no buffers and an auto coupler is seen in the works yard painted in workshops primer at Leeds awaiting shipping to the Daina Oil Refinery in Baghdad, Iraq in April 1956.* Author's collection

The Diesel Shunter

North British Loco Co 0-4-0 diesel-hydraulic
11700-11707
D2700-D2707

The North British Locomotive Co of Glasgow, which was a major player in the construction of steam traction, was faced with a total change in the early to mid-1950s with a trend from most countries around the world towards 'modern', non-steam, traction. NBL was keen to remain in the construction field and answered the tender documentation of the BTC.

As NBL was not involved with and not interested in diesel-electric technology, it decided to follow the trend towards diesel-hydraulic transmission of continental Europe. To do this they entered a license agreement with German engineering giant Voith.

Many people consider that the policy of NBL to steer towards diesel-hydraulic transmissions was the start of the decline of the company, for just at the time when NBL was refining diesel-hydraulic transmissions and performance, BR announced it was to adopt the diesel-electric transmission as its standard.

As part of the early dieselisation of the Hartlepool Docks yards, BR ordered a fleet of three 0-4-0 locomotives in 1951; these were almost of a steam outline and numbered 11700-11702, emerging from the NBL Queen's Park Works between July 1953 and August 1954. In early 1954, five additional locomotives were

ordered for use in Scottish yards and these emerged between August 1955 and February 1956.

The design of the follow-on order was slightly different from that of the first three, which had a 'bunker' style design on the rear of the cab. The follow-on order also had a stepped height bonnet and revised radiator panels.

The locomotives were powered by a 200hp Paxman 6RPH engine, which in collaboration with the Voith L33YV transmission did not give all that good a performance.

No train braking was originally provided, but locomotives from the second batch were modified in the 1960s with vacuum brake equipment.

When delivered the entire fleet was finished in standard diesel black livery, off-set by a Lion over Wheel logo on the cab side above the number. Locomotives were later repainted into standard green livery, when a standard British Railways Lion over Crown logo was applied to the cab side.

In common with many of the other smaller shunter designs, this fleet became surplus to requirements due to the changing needs of the rail industry. Withdrawal from service came in 1963 for the pioneer locomotive, with the remainder being taken out of stock in 1967-68, and all were broken up for scrap.

Below: *The final locomotive of the original order for three 0-4-0 diesel-hydraulic locomotives, No 11702, emerged from the Queens Park works in Glasgow in mid-July 1954. The locomotive was allocated to West Hartlepool for dock working and was delivered via Darlington Works, where this illustration was taken on 25 July. No 11702 took up operation in the first week of August 1954. The livery shown is BR black.* **H. M. Brown**

BR 1948 number range:	11700-11707
BR 1957 number range:	D2700-D2707
Built by:	NBL Glasgow
Years introduced:	1953-1956
Wheel arrangement:	0-4-0
Weight: D2700-D2702 -	31 tons
D2703-D2707 -	32 tons
Height: D2700-D2702 -	12ft 0in
D2703-D2707 -	11ft 6in
Length: D2700-D2702 -	22ft 11½in
D2703-D2707 -	22ft 9¾in
Width:	8ft 6in
Wheelbase:	6ft 0in
Wheel diameter:	3ft 6in
Min curve negotiable:	1 chain
Engine type:	Paxman 6RPH
Engine output:	200hp
Power at rail:	140hp
Tractive effort:	21,500lb
Cylinder bore:	7in
Cylinder stroke:	7¼in
Maximum speed:	
D2700-D2702 -	14mph
D2703-D2707 -	12mph
Brake type:	
D2700-D2702 -	Air on loco, no train brakes
D2703-D2707 -	Air on loco, vacuum train brakes (fitted later)
Brake force:	16 tons
Route availability:	1
Heating type:	Not fitted
Multiple coupling type:	Not fitted
Transmission type:	Hydraulic — Voith L33YV
Fuel tank capacity:	155gal
Cooling water capacity:	48gal
Lub oil capacity:	12gal
Sanding equipment:	Pneumatic

Below: *The official 'works profile' view of the first member of the class No 11700. The picture is likely to have been taken during its acceptance inspection and commissioning at Darlington Works around July 1953. 11700 was allocated new to Hartlepool Docks on 13 July 1953. Note the traditional North British Locomotive Co diamond shaped works plate below the Lion over Wheel crest on the cab side.* **D Porter collection**

The Diesel Shunter

Right: *The first three locomotives of the fleet were significantly different from the remainder of the fleet, which had a much improved body design. The first three had a steam outline, complete with 'bunker' to the rear of the cab. No 11701 is seen 'on shed' at Darlington on 6 October 1957. This locomotive was delivered new on 23 November 1953 to Hartlepool Docks. It was withdrawn in March 1967 and broken up by Draper's of Hull the same year.*
B. K. B. Green

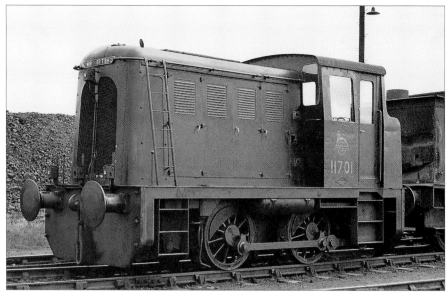

Left: *The pioneer of the fleet, No 11700 was renumbered to D2700 on 17 February 1958, and for a while carried a small size 'D' prefix. With the revised Lion over Crown emblem, the locomotive is seen at Darlington on 20 September 1959.* **A. Swain**

Below: *Not long after introduction, single-note warning horns were fitted towards the front end of the bonnet roof, seen here on No 11702 apparently out of service at Darlington Works on 10 May 1959. It is worth noting the fold-down chromium plated foot grips just in front of the cab.*
Norman Preedy

The Diesel Shunter

Above: *The second batch of locomotives all went to the Scottish Region and had a more pleasing body profile, as shown on No 11705, viewed from its nose end at South Leith, Edinburgh on 22 April 1957. The locomotive shows its 'as delivered' black livery, with red buffer beam and white painted running number.* R. E. Vincent

Left: *Renumbered to D2704 from 11704 in December 1959, the locomotive is seen at Dunfermline on 10 May 1966. By this time the locomotive had been repainted BR locomotive green and had gained yellow/black wasp warning ends. To meet the then 'modern' requirements, vacuum train brakes were also installed, but frontal illumination was still only by an oil lamp.* P. Foster

Right: *Standing 'on shed' at Edinburgh St Margarets on 6 August 1959, No 11706 is seen with the front door of its radiator compartment removed for maintenance. The locomotive, is in BTC black livery and was delivered on 29 December 1955. It spent its entire working life of 12 years allocated in the Edinburgh area. On withdrawal it was sold to Slag Reduction in Ickles, South Yorkshire and broken up in August 1967.* A. Swain

The Diesel Shunter

North British Loco Co 0-4-0 diesel-hydraulic 11708-11719 D2708-D2780

Through the mid 1950s, the Glasgow-based North British Locomotive Co continued its development of the use of diesel-hydraulic locomotives. Eventually the company obtained a license to use the German built MAN diesel engine coupled to a Voith transmission. From this partnership agreement emerged a well-designed 0-4-0 locomotive.

Compared with earlier NBL shunting locomotives (11700-11707), these locomotives had a much improved general arrangement and cab layout.

Although the eventual production run covered 73 locos, the initial order placed by the BR in 1955 was for just 12 machines, which emerged from July 1957 and were initially allocated to the Scottish Region; all were delivered by the end of 1957.

Concurrent with the first order, the BR placed a follow-on order for 61 locos, which were delivered from June 1958 through until March 1961 and again were all allocated to the Scottish Region. The structural design for this follow-on order was slightly different, with a slightly longer body and 3ft 9in diameter wheels compared to 3ft 6in on the first batch. The front radiator panel was also slightly amended. Structurally the earlier-built 12 locomotives were always identifiable in having an extra plate-mounted box directly in front of the cab section on the left side.

The first 12 locomotives were numbered 11708-11719 in the 1948 series; these were renumbered to D2708-D2719 from the early 1960s. The follow-on order emerged carrying numbers D2720-D2780.

The first examples were painted from new in BR black, offset by a Lion over Wheel logo on the engine compartment side, the running number being applied to the cab side. On at least three of the first batch, front end warning livery trials using various configurations of white and black and yellow and black were tried to gauge the effect on track workers. The follow-on locomotives were all painted in standard locomotive green livery from new, together with a standard Lion over crown British Railways motif. Standard yellow/black chevron warning ends were also applied.

These locomotives were all fitted with train vacuum brakes from new, together with straight air brakes for locomotive use. Front and rear electric marker lights were standard.

Most of the fleet remained working in Scotland for their entire lives, with withdrawals taking place between January 1967 and February 1968. A small number of locomotives were transferred to Crewe and Wolverton Works for pilot operations.

Two locomotives, Nos D2767/74, have thankfully been saved from the cutters torch and are both preserved on the East Lancs Railway.

Left: The subject of high-visibility warning ends of shunting traction arose in mid-1957 and authorisation was given for several locomotives of different designs to have trial warning ends applied. NBL No 11709 was one such locomotive, seen here when new painted in BTC black livery with Lion over Wheel logo sporting white/black warning lines on the nose end. This locomotive, allocated new to Dundee, also has a yellow lined red buffer beam. The illustration was taken at St Rollox on 27 August 1957.
Peter Groom

Right: Broadside study of No 11718, delivered new to Dunfermline on 30 October 1957 and the penultimate locomotive of the class to be delivered with a 1948-series number. Compared with the view above, this illustration shows the other side of the locomotive and shows that on the driving side running plate an additional equipment box was located. It is interesting to note the angled shield to the front of the footstep covering the jackshaft drive. The distinctive NBL diamond makers plate is clearly visible. No 11718 is seen at its home depot.
D. C. Smith

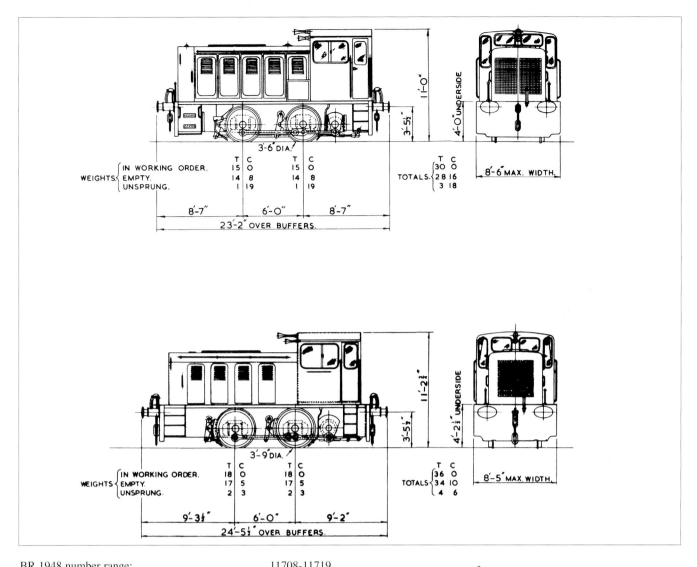

BR 1948 number range:	11708-11719	-
BR 1957 number range:	D2708-D2719	D2720-D2780
Former class code:	DY11, later D2/10, 2/4	DY, later 2/10, 2/4B
Built by:	NBL Glasgow	NBL Glasgow
Years introduced:	1957	1958-1961
Wheel arrangement:	0-4-0	0-4-0
Weight:	30 tons	36 tons
Height:	11ft 0in	11ft 2³/4in
Length:	23ft 2in	24ft 5¹/2in
Width:	8ft 6in	8ft 5in
Wheelbase:	6ft 0in	6ft 0in
Wheel diameter:	3ft 6in	3ft 9in
Min curve negotiable:	1¹/2 chains	1 ¹/2 chains
Engine type:	NBL-MAN W6V 17.5/22A	NBL-MAN W6V 17.5/22A
Engine output:	225hp	225hp
Power at rail:	180hp	180hp
Tractive effort:	20,080lb	21,500lb
Cylinder bore:	7in	7in
Cylinder stroke:	7¹/2in	7¹/2in
Maximum speed:	15mph	17mph
Brake type:	Air on loco, vacuum train brakes	Air on loco, vacuum train brakes
Brake force:	15 tons	17 tons
Route availability:	1	1
Heating type:	Not fitted	Not fitted
Multiple coupling type:	Not fitted	Not fitted
Transmission type:	Hydraulic — Voith L33YV	Hydraulic — Voith L33YV
Fuel tank capacity:	225gal	300gal
Cooling water capacity:	45gal	45gal
Lub oil capacity:	12gal	12gal
Sanding equipment:	Pneumatic	Pneumatic

The Diesel Shunter

Left & Middle: *These two illustrations clearly show the structural differences between the two builds forming this class. No D2711 left top depicts the body style on the first 12 locomotives, having a straight top engine compartment and four removable bodyside doors. The middle illustration, of No D2760, shows the body style on the main production run of 61 locomotives, fitted with a raised engine compartment hood just to the front of the cab and only three hinged and removable body side doors. The pictures also show two different styles of wasp warning ends, and a white painted running number on the buffer beam of locomotive No D2760. Both: CJM collection*

Below: *By the time some of the later examples of this 0-4-0 class emerged from the Queen's Park Works of North British Locomotive Co in Glasgow, the yellow/black wasp warning end had been accepted as standard and was applied from new. No D2754 is seen at Edinburgh St Margarets shed on 11 June 1960 painted in standard BR locomotive green. J. P. Cornish*

Above: *The nose end of BR green-liveried locomotives, dressed with the wasp ends looked very smart, with the yellow colour being applied to the movable radiator fins on the end. No D2755, complete with number on the front buffer beam, is seen when new. This locomotive was delivered from NBL on 11 May 1960 and shedded at Dalry Road.* Norman E .Preedy

Right: *Painted in standard BR locomotive green livery with the later BR Lion over Crown logo on the cabside, No D2723 is seen in one of the turntable stabling roads at Edinburgh St Margarets shed on 14 September 1959. This locomotive was delivered to the BR on 30 June 1958.* B. A. Hill

Right: *In resplendent condition, No D2758, stands on shed at Glasgow Eastfield on 19 June 1960. This view gives a perfect modellers guide to the front end equipment, including detail of the cast North British makers plate on the nose end above the radiator. It is interesting to see that a standard oil-powered locomotive headlight is fitted, even though electric marker lights were installed.* Gavin Morrison

The Diesel Shunter

Yorkshire Engine Co 0-4-0 diesel-hydraulic
D2850-D2869
Class 02
02001-02004

Subsequent to the mid-1950s orders for replacement traction, the BRB had an ongoing need for very small wheelbase 'modern' shunting or pilot locomotives towards the end of the decade and placed an order for 20 six-foot wheelbase 170hp diesel hydraulic locos.

To many this very distinctive design of shunting locomotive, perhaps one of the more handsome of the earlier builds, was a direct replacement for the Lancashire & Yorkshire 0-4-0ST 'Pugs' and to this end the Yorkshire Engine Co machines, classified originally as D1/4, were principally deployed on Merseyside and in the Manchester area. It was the specification of the 1890 built 'Pugs', that was actually given to Yorkshire Engine Co when this fleet was ordered. Not being delivered until the autumn of 1960, the fleet was allocated 'D' numbers in the 1957 series in the range D2850-D2869.

The first locomotive to emerge from the builders works, No D2850 was delivered in September and allocated to Bank Hall, Liverpool; after three locomotives had been delivered, Longsight (Manchester) received No D2853, but after this deliveries reverted to Bank Hall, with some machines being delivered to Newton Heath, Accrington and one, No D2859, to Burton. All locomotives were delivered by December 1961.

At the time this order was placed, diesel hydraulic transmissions were still favoured for shunting, and indeed main line power, and the prime mover sanctioned for this build was the Rolls Royce C6 six cylinder unit, set to deliver just 170hp, providing a tractive effort of 15,000lb. The power unit and associated Rolls Royce torque converter and transmission assembly were slightly inclined towards the cab end, with the drive powering the wheelset below the driving cab.

The body style of the small machines was one of the best designed of any of the early diesel types. In a break from usual UK design, access to the cab was not from the sides, but from a full-width verandah, or balcony across the back, fenced in by handrails more in keeping with North American practice. This design was also used on the small 0-4-0 Brush prototypes (D2999 and D9998).

The locomotives' performance was reported to be good, especially in the Liverpool dock complex lines, where their size and light weight, at just 28 tons, permitted their use virtually anywhere, including on some of the small wagon turntables found in limited-clearance shed and terminal buildings.

Although fitted with a hydraulic transmission, which fell out of favour with the British Railways Board in the mid-1960s, this fleet remained intact until 1969, when some members were withdrawn, mainly due to loss of work rather than unreliability. Four members Nos D2851-3/6, remained in traffic long enough to be allocated TOPS numbers in 1973, although only three (Nos 02001/3/4) were actually so numbered.

The final demise for the class came in mid-1975, with many locomotives entering industrial use and eventually preservation. However one locomotive, No D2860 when withdrawn in December 1970 from Allerton was placed in long term store with the eventual plan to see the locomotive preserved. In a period when the word preservation was seen as unpleasant within the BRB, it is quite remarkable that this locomotive survived. It was stored at various locations including Brighton until 1978 when it was sent to Thomas Hill and refurbished. After this it was officially claimed as part of the National collection and is now used as an in-museum pilot at the National Railway Museum, York. Here its small size is very useful, being able to operate to all parts of the complex and take exhibits onto the turntable with ease.

The fleet was built with vacuum train brakes from new and the livery applied was standard locomotive green, off-set by black and yellow angled warning ends. Electric marker lights were provided on both ends and the second style, Lion over Crown logo was carried on the cab side.

Left: Built as a direct replacement for the Lancashire & Yorkshire 0-4-0ST 'Pugs', these Yorkshire Engine Co machines, classified originally as D1/4, were principally deployed on Merseyside and in the Manchester area. Delivered in BR standard locomotive green livery, complete with yellow/black wasp ends, these were some of the most unusual of the small shunters, having a balcony cab entrance. No D2852 is seen parked on a wagon turntable in this official view. CJM collection

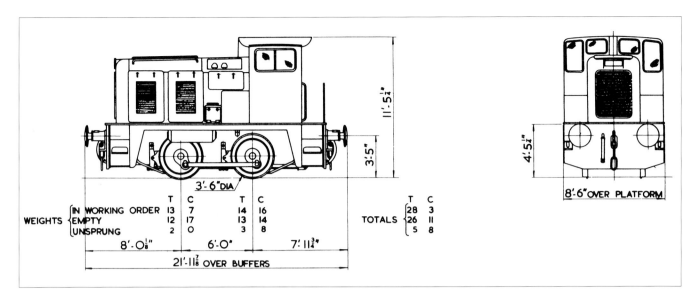

TOPS number range:	02001-02004 (not all renumbered)		Cylinder bore:	5¹/₈in
1957 BR number range:	D2850-D2869		Cylinder stroke:	6in
Former class codes:	D1/4, later 1/17		Maximum speed:	19¹/₂mph
Built by:	Yorkshire Eng Co		Brake type:	Air on loco, vacuum train brakes
Years introduced:	1960-1961		Brake force:	21 tons
Wheel arrangement:	0-4-0		Route availability:	1
Weight:	28 tons 3 cwt		Heating type:	Not fitted
Height:	11ft 5¹/₄in		Multiple coupling type:	Not fitted
Length:	21ft 11⁷/₈in		Transmission:	Hydraulic
Width:	8ft 6in			Engine-gearbox — Rolls Royce
Wheelbase:	6ft 0in			Gearbox — Rolls Royce
Wheel diameter:	3ft 6in			Final drive — Yorkshire Eng Co
Min curve negotiable:	1 chain		Fuel tank capacity:	300gal
Engine type:	Rolls Royce C6		Cooling water capacity:	36gal
Engine output:	170hp at 1,800rpm		Lub oil capacity:	11gal
Power at rail:	100hp		Sanding equipment:	Pneumatic
Tractive effort:	15,000lb			

Below: Yorkshire Engine Co body ends. The illustration below left shows the distinctive cab balcony or verandah end, with just one access to the cab via a central door. The illustration below right shows the nose or radiator end. Equipment consisted of four marker lights, three fitted to the top lip of the buffer beam and the other on the bodywork. Buffer beam equipment consists of a shackle coupling and a vacuum pipe. Locomotive No D2852 is illustrated. Both: CJM collection.

Right: *Viewed from its cab end, No D2869 is seen at Allerton on 28 July 1968. This locomotive was delivered new to Bank Hall shed on 9 December 1961 and remained working at Liverpool Docks until transferred to Reddish depot in Manchester, where it stayed until withdrawn on 14 December 1969. The locomotive was disposed of at T W Ward at Beighton in mid-1971.*
M. Gascoyne

Left: *Viewed from its non-driving side is No D2868 at Allerton depot. Both sides of the locomotives were of similar outline, with that on the drivers side having a recessed section directly in front of the cab. Fuel tanks were located on both sides, attached to the running plate directly in front of the cab. Visibility from these locomotives was good, with a well raised cab section offering a good view over the angled bonnet section.*
A. Roberts

Right: *This Yorkshire Engine Co fleet remained in traffic long enough to be awarded a numeric TOPS classification — 02 and indeed three locomotives were actually renumbered into the Class 02 prefixed fleet. Standing between duties with a Class 08, No D2857, looking rather the worse for wear, is seen at Allerton depot in April 1971.*
Norman Preedy

The Diesel Shunter

This page: *Thankfully, one locomotive of this class was saved from disposal and taken on-board by the National collection. After a period of store in the old Pullman shed at Brighton, No D2860 was taken to the then-new National Railway Museum, York. Having been restored, it is one of the Museum pilots and is still frequently used to shunt exhibits around the complex. In the view above, the locomotive is seen on the turntable of the Great Hall during a shunt manoeuvre to take in a new exhibit. The view below, shows the locomotive pulling ex-LNER 'V2' No 4771* **Green Arrow** *out of the Museum workshop.*
Both: **Colin J. Marsden**

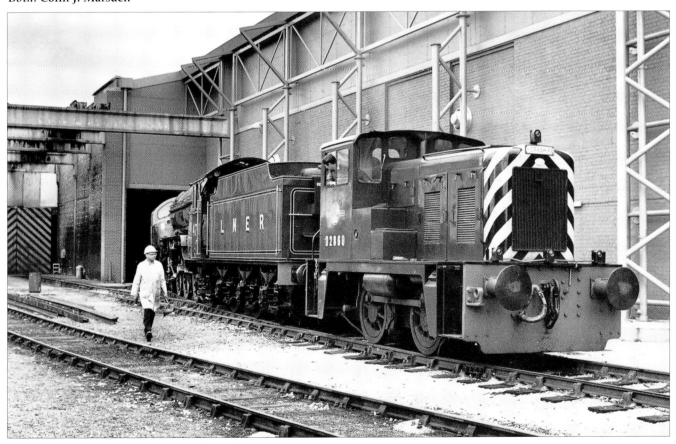

The Diesel Shunter

North British Loco 0-4-0 diesel-hydraulic D2900-D2913

Another of the follow-on orders placed subsequently by the BTC after the modernisation batch of orders, was for this fleet of North British 330hp 0-4-0 machines. The initial order was for 11 locomotives, allocated numbers D2900-D2910 and NBL works numbers 27751-27761, which was followed by a repeat order for three locomotives Nos D2911-D2913 (NBL Works Nos 27995-27997). The final three locomotives were to a very slightly different design.

The fleet was again designed to replace steam traction on dock and limited clearance lines, including docksides, depots and works sidings. The locomotives were built to typical NBL design at the Queens Park Works in Glasgow from late in 1957, with the first locomotive emerging in April 1958. Between then and September, Nos D2900-D2907 were delivered to Devons Road shed in Bow, London and finally ousted steam traction for pilot workings, replacing the Fowler 3F 0-6-0Ts. The decision to deploy these locomotives at Bow was a direct result of the London Clean Air Act, which required the number of steam locomotives working in East London to be reduced as quickly as possible.

After the eight locomotives were delivered to Devons Road, three examples went to Rugby, one to Nuneaton and two to Edge Hill. The main order for eleven was completed in October 1958 with the three follow-on members being delivered together in December 1959.

For their size these were remarkably powerful locomotives, developing 330hp, only just a shade less than the BR standard 0-6-0 of Class 08. The prime mover installed was a German design MAN unit of type W6V, assembled in the UK under the North British/MAN partnership license agreement. In common with other diesel-hydraulic locomotives of the period the licence deal also covered the transmission assembly of the Voith L24V type.

The traditional-design single cab structure had a slightly raised cab section offering good all-round visibility, driver and crew access was by hinged doors on either side, with the driving controls facing the power unit end, but arranged for easy operation facing either direction. The engine or bonnet section was slightly narrower than full width and had five hinged and removable doors giving access to the engine and control equipments. By the time this design of locomotive was finalised train brakes were a stipulation and vacuum brakes were fitted from new. Air brakes were used on the loco.

The nose end of the locomotive housed the radiator or cooler group, with a mesh central section to the bonnet end. Electric marker lights were provided on both nose and cab ends.

The very minor structural differences of the final three locomotives saw the overall length reduced by around one inch, while a minor technical upgrade to the power unit and transmission was made.

While these locomotives performed well with few 'on-line' failures, the decision made by the BRB to opt for all diesel-electric transmissions, saw these diesel-hydraulic machines doomed from an early date. Deployment of the fleet changed with the introduction of new classes and by the mid 1960s the first five fleet members were allocated to Crewe and Wolverton works for pilot operations, while the remainder remained on the books of the LMR. The entire fleet were withdrawn from the February stock changes in 1967, one of the rare occasions a complete class was withdrawn 'en block'. The entire fleet was sold to one scrap dealer, Slag Reduction of Ickles, where disposal was made between September-December of the same year.

When introduced the fleet was finished in standard BR locomotive green, with cream locomotive number applied to the cab side, complete with the 'D' prefix. Below the number was the British Railways logo.

During the early 1960s yellow/black wasp ends were applied. Buffer beams were finished in red.

Below: These powerful 0-4-0 diesel-hydraulic locomotives shared allocation between the Eastern and London Midland Regions and were well-liked by the staff. On 27 June 1959, No D2910 of the second order is seen shunting bogie parcels stock at Coventry. It is painted in BR green livery. **Michael Mensing**

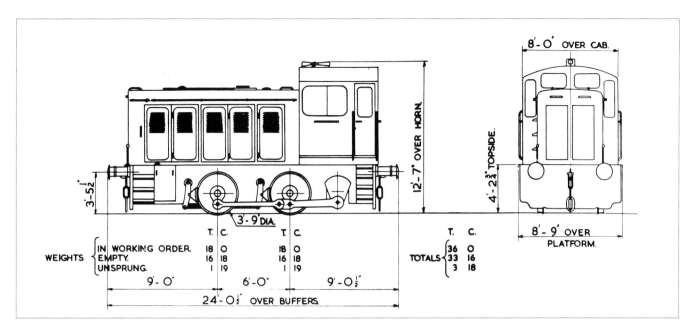

			T.	C.	
			18	0	
WEIGHTS	IN WORKING ORDER.		18	0	
	EMPTY.		16	18	
	UNSPRUNG.		1	19	

WEIGHTS { IN WORKING ORDER. 18|0 18|0   TOTALS { 36|0
 EMPTY. 16|18 16|18 33|16
 UNSPRUNG. 1|19 1|19 3|18

BR 1957 number range:	D2900-D2913
Former class code:	D3/1, later 3/4
Built by:	NBL Glasgow
Years introduced:	1958-1959
Wheel arrangement:	0-4-0
Weight:	36 tons
Height:	12ft 7in
Length:	D2900-D2910 - 24ft 0$^1/_2$in
	D2911-D2913 - 23ft 11$^1/_2$in
Width:	8ft 9in
Wheelbase:	6ft 0in
Wheel diameter:	3ft 9in
Min curve negotiable:	1 chain
Engine type:	NBL-MAN W6V 17.5/22AS
Engine output:	330hp

Power at rail:	270hp
Tractive effort:	20,160lb
Cylinder bore:	7in
Cylinder stroke:	7$^1/_2$in
Maximum speed:	20mph
Brake type:	Air on loco, vacuum train brakes
Brake force:	18 tons
Route availability:	1
Heating type:	Not fitted
Multiple coupling type:	Not fitted
Transmission type:	Hydraulic — Voith L24V
Fuel tank capacity:	450gal
Cooling water capacity:	40
Lub oil capacity:	12
Sanding equipment:	Pneumatic

Right: *The official North British Locomotive Company view of No, D2903, viewed from the cab end, drivers side. The livery is standard BR locomotive green, off-set by a yellow lined, red buffer beam. Running numbers are applied in white, with a standard British Railways logo below. This locomotive was delivered in April 1958 and allocated new to Devons Road shed.* **Author's collection**

Above: Two eras of shunting power pose side by side in East London. On the left is new No D2907, delivered to Devons Road shed on 16 August 1958, while on the right is LMS 'Jinty' 0-6-0T No 47517. The working environment for footplate staff was considerably improved with the introduction of diesel shunting power, but the visibility from the cab was not a major advance. In many areas, the deployment of diesel shunting power was used as an attempt to introduce single manning of shunting locomotives, but in the main this was not supported by the drivers' trade union.
Author's collection

Below: In common with other designs of diesel shunting power, these NBL machines had a number of side opening and removable doors, each with a ventilation grille. These gave access to the prime mover and transmission. With its cab end on the right, No D2902 is viewed from the driver's side in this picture taken at Devons Road shed in Bow, London.
F. Hornby

The Diesel Shunter

Above: *By the time this fleet of diesel-hydraulic locomotives was ordered, vacuum train braking was a standard fitting, as identified by the presence of a vacuum pipe on the buffer beam. However at the time of introduction the vast majority of stock was still un-braked. On 31 July 1962, No D2908 is seen shunting a rake of wooden- and steel-bodied coal wagons with a brake van in the middle at Rugby.* **M. Norman**

Below: *No D2905, delivered in June 1958 to Devons Road depot, is viewed from the non-driving or 'second mans' side. On this side of the locomotive's bonnet section, the second inspection door from the cab end is of a slightly different design, incorporating a square section grille. As can be seen, air-controlled windscreen wipers were provided on the forward/rear facing main windows. Extra forward vision was provided by two horizontal windows overlooking the main bonnet section. D2905 is seen stored at Wolverton Works on 6 September 1967.* **Peter Groom**

Hunslet Eng Co 0-4-0 diesel-mechanical 11500-11502 D2950-D2952

The Hunslet Engine Co of Leeds, answered a specific design requirement of the BTC in 1953, when three small 5ft 6in wheelbase, 0-4-0 diesel-mechanical shunting locomotives were ordered for dock and tramway use.

Since Nationalisation in 1948, the Eastern Region had operated several mainly agricultural lines in East Anglia, where the railway tracks ran over public roadways, mainly to gain access to shipping ports. The most notable was at Ipswich, where a tramway network ran between the main line and the dockside.

Under modernisation plans, the operation of 'modern traction' over such lines needed special consideration and locomotives fitted with 'skirts' to protect the moving parts of the wheelsets and running gear were needed. These were basically a 'cowcatcher' at front and rear and hinged side flaps.

The small fleet of dock shunters had to have a very short wheelbase as the curvature in the dock areas was very restricted.

BR, in conjunction with Hunslet, designed this class to overcome the problems. The three locomotives were delivered, painted in black livery in December 1954 and January 1955 and were allocated to 32B — Ipswich shed. The locomotives were of typical Hunslet design, with a roomy driving cab providing good all round visibility. The locomotives were fitted with straight air brakes for their own braking, but no train brakes were provided. Electric front and rear marker lights were fitted from new.

In original as-delivered condition, the locomotives were numbered in the 1948 five digit system as 11500-11502. From 1957 the fleet was renumbered D2950-D2952. Locomotives repainted in the early 1960s emerged in BR standard locomotive green, with yellow/black chevron warning ends. Originally the Lion over Wheel logo was used, this changing on BR green with the standard British Railways Lion over Crown logo. No locomotive remained in service long enough to receive BR blue livery and no TOPS classification was given.

When the Ipswich tramway system closed in December 1966, all three were stored at Ipswich. In 1967 two locomotives (D2950/1) were transferred to Goole, again for dock use, while No D2952 was withdrawn in 1966 for scrap. The first two locomotives of the build were withdrawn at the end of 1967, with the pioneer locomotive going into industrial service with Thyssen of Llanelly and eventually being broken up in 1983.

Below: Following the old steam-era tradition of painting the first locomotive of each build in workshop grey primer for official pictures, this is Hunslet's 'official' illustration of No 11500, taken in the Leeds factory in October 1954, just prior to final painting and branding for delivery to Ipswich depot in December. Being destined for use in the Ipswich tramway and dock system, full side protection and cowcatchers were fitted, more resembling armour plating than protection for the public. **CJM collection**

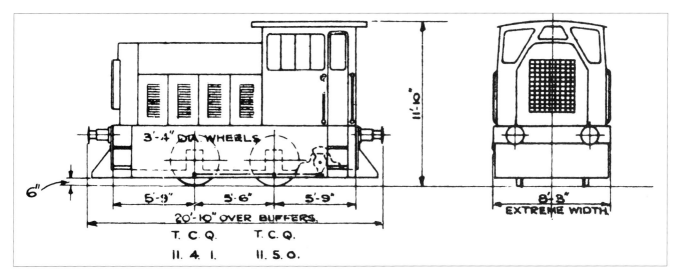

BR 1948 number range:	11500-11502	Power at rail:	107hp
BR 1957 number range:	D2950-D2952	Tractive effort:	10,800lb
Former class code:	DY1, later D1/1 and 1/15	Cylinder	5$\frac{1}{2}$in
Built by:	Hunslet Engine Co	Cylinder stroke:	7$\frac{3}{4}$in
Year introduced:	1954-1955	Maximum speed:	14mph
Wheel arrangement:	0-4-0	Brake type:	Air on loco, no train brakes
Weight:	23 tons	Brake force:	13 tons
Height:	11ft 10in	Route availability:	1
Length:	20ft 10in	Heating type:	Not fitted
Width	8ft 3in	Multiple coupling type:	Not fitted
Wheelbase	5ft 6in	Transmission type:	Mechanical — Hunslet 4 speed
Wheel diameter:	3ft 4in	Fuel tank capacity:	100gal
Min curve negotiable:	1 chain	Cooling water capacity:	40
Engine type:	Gardner 6L3	Lub oil capacity:	13
Engine output:	153hp	Sanding equipment:	Pneumatic

Below: *By now painted in BR black livery, No 11500 is seen in July 1956.* **CJM collection**

Above: *In early January 1955, 'small' Hunslet No 11500 shunts wagon stock in Ipswich Docks, in the background is 'large' Hunslet No 11136. As can be seen from the lack of connections of the buffer beam, these 'small' Hunslets were not fitted with train brakes, all braking being achieved by the locomotive direct air brakes.* CJM collection

Right: *Taken from the opposite side to the above illustration, No 11500 is seen in the dock complex at Ipswich on 6 September 1955. The presence of 'cow-catchers' on the front ends prevented easy access to the drawgear for shunting staff, with the shackle laying at an angle on a wooden 'plate' to avoid rattling.* A. O'Hear

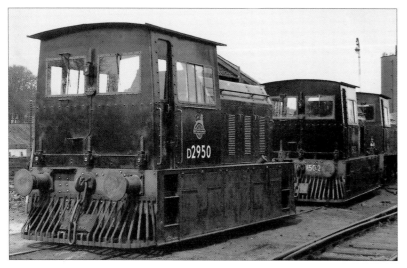

Left: *A quite remarkable illustration taken at Ipswich in late April 1958 shows No D2950 (11500) from the cab end displaying its early 1957 number with a small 'D', and No 11502 still to be renumbered as D2952. Note that a powered windscreen wiper was only installed on the driver's side end window. In front of the two 'small' Hunslets, is one of the larger 0-6-0 Hunslet diesel locos.* CJM collection

Right: *By the late 1950s, repaints found the three locomotives sporting BR standard green livery, offset progressively by wasp warning ends and the standard BR Lion over Crown logo on the cab side. Looking rather decrepit, No D2951 is seen at Ipswich Docks on 4 August 1960.*
F. L. Marsland

Below: *Obviously out of service, the pioneer of the fleet No 11500 or D2950 in seen with its four body side inspection doors removed to give access to the Gardner power unit at Yarmouth shed around summer 1959.*
P. J. Sharpe

Below: *Running through the streets of Ipswich Docks, where the underframe running gear protection was needed to stop members of the public getting tangled up in wheels and motion, No D2951 is seen on 4 August 1960, painted in BR green livery and sporting standard 'wasp' warning ends. All three of the 'small' Hunslets were taken out of service at Ipswich and stored in December 1966, this locomotive being subsequently reinstated to Goole in January 1967 for a further 12 months service.*
F. L. Marsland

The Diesel Shunter

Andrew Barclay 0-4-0 diesel-mechanical
11503-11506, D2953-D2956
Class 01
01001-01002

These four, six-foot wheelbase 0-4-0 diesel-mechanical units were order by the BTC as part of the shunter replacement scheme in 1955. The mechanical parts were built by Andrew Barclay of Kilmarnock, using a small 153hp Gardner 6-cylinder engine. The locomotives were allocated the numbers 11503-11506 and were classified as DY2.

The four locomotives were designed to replace small 0-4-0 steam locomotives used on very restrictive dock and workshop lines. In common with many other like designs of the period no train braking was provided. The structural design was very 'Andrew Barclay' with a raised centre section of the engine compartment directly in front of the cab and a small 'bonnet' protruding from the cab end. In many ways these were just a smaller, scaled-down version of the 0-6-0s numbered in the 11177-86 (D2400-D2409) series.

The four locomotives under review here emerged between January and March 1956 and were allocated to Stratford shed in East London, interesting feature of the design being a wooden cab door and a very basic driving cab. The small fleet remained in the Stratford area for several years, working on some of the dock complex lines around East London, but were most frequently seen in and around Stratford depot and works.

Under the British Transport Commission's National Traction Plan, classes such as this had little hope for survival. However, due to their small size and quite good performance when compared with other early classes, two locomotives were found further use in the mid-1960s, working on the isolated Holyhead Breakwater line in Anglesey. It is even more remarkable to record that the pair selected for this re-allocation, Nos D2954/55 were still painted in 1950s BR black livery in the mid-1960s when re-allocation took place. As the pair were still on the books in 1973 when TOPS renumbering was introduced, they were classified as Class 01 and allocated the numbers 01001 and 01002, although by this time No 01001 was technically out of use, but was not withdrawn until 1979.

Work on the isolated Holyhead line kept No 01002 busy until 1981, when the system closed. At the time No 01001 was still present providing spare parts for its operational sister for many years. Sadly both locomotives were broken up at Holyhead in February 1982.

When withdrawn from use at Stratford in 1966/7 the other two members of the fleet were not sold for industrial use. No D2953 went to Thames Matex of West Thurrock in Essex and was later sold into preservation and is now at Peak Rail. No D2956 eventually went to King's scrapyard in Snailwell Suffolk and was later rescued by preservationists and is now on the East Lancashire Railway.

An interesting twist to this fleet is that a fifth locomotive of the same design was built in 1958 for departmental use as No 81, being allocated to Peterborough. This locomotive was slightly modified in that it had steel cab doors and rubber gromitted windows. After its useful departmental operation was over, the locomotive was offered to the capital stock fleet, where it was taken into stock as the second No D2956 in July 1967, the first having been withdrawn in May 1966.

The second No D2956 did not remain in service for long, being withdrawn in November 1967 from Doncaster depot, going for industrial use at the British Steel Corporation, Briton Ferry.

In terms of livery, these locomotives were always painted BR black, with the early version of the Lion over Wheel logo. Once on the Holyhead Breakwater, an unusual form of yellow black wasp end was applied, using horizontal alternate bands, as shown in the illustrations. Front and cab end equipment consisted of the usual buffers, originally round units were applied, but these later gave way to oval head assemblies. A standard coupling hook and link shackle was installed. End illumination was provided by four electric marker lights, three at buffer beam height and one on the cab back/radiator top. The two locomotives used on the Holyhead system acquired a rather unusual wooden lower extension to the buffer beam.

Right: *Delivered on the last day of March 1956, Andrew Barclay 'small' 0-4-0 No 11506 is seen 'on shed' at Stratford East London when just nine months old. The locomotive is seen in black livery. These locomotives were not fitted with automatic fuelling connections, with diesel oil literally poured into the blister tank in front of the cab, hence the spill of fuel down the bodyside.*
Derek Porter

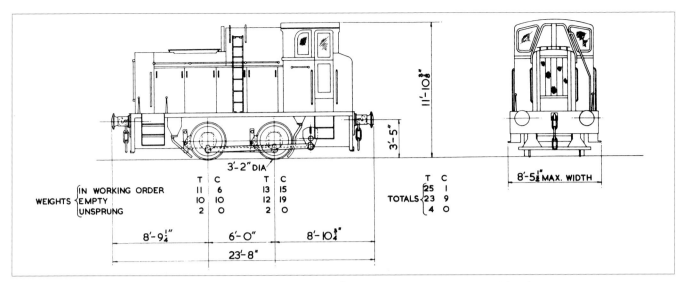

WEIGHTS		T	C		T	C
	IN WORKING ORDER	11	6		13	15
	EMPTY	10	10		12	19
	UNSPRUNG	2	0		2	0

TOTALS	T	C
	25	1
	23	9
	4	0

3'-2" DIA

8'-9¼" 6'-0" 8'-10¾"

23'-8"

11'-10⅜" 3'-5"

8'-5½" MAX. WIDTH

TOPS number range:	01001-01002	Maximum speed:	14¼mph
1948 BR number range:	11503-11506	Brake type:	Air on loco, no train brakes
1957 BR number range:	D2953-D2956 (Note: 1)	Brake force:	15 tons
Former class codes:	DY1, later D1/2, 1/12	Route availability:	1
Built by:	Andrew Barclay, Kilmarnock	Heating type:	Not fitted
Year introduced:	1956 (Note: 2)	Multiple coupling type:	Not fitted
Wheel arrangement:	0-4-0	Transmission:	Mechanical
Weight:	25 tons 1 cwt		Engine-gearbox — Vulcan Sinclair
Height	11ft 10³/₈in		Gearbox — Wilson 4-speed SE4
Length:	23ft 8in		Final drive — Wiseman 15RLGB
Width:	8ft 5in	Fuel tank capacity:	325gal
Wheelbase	6ft 0in	Cooling water capacity:	35gal
Wheel diameter:	3ft 2in	Lub oil capacity:	12gal
Min curve negotiable:	1.06 chains	Sanding equipment:	Pneumatic
Engine type:	Gardner 6L3		
Engine output:	153hp		
Power at rail:	102hp		
Tractive effort:	12,750lb		
Cylinder bore:	5¹/₂in		
Cylinder stroke:	7³/₄in		

Notes
1. Departmental No 81 later taken into capital stock as D2956, after original locomotive withdrawn.
2. D2956 became Class 01 in 1967.

Right: *Viewed from the opposite side to the picture of the same locomotive on the opposite page, No 11506 is again seen at Stratford, this time on 16 June 1958. The main difference on this side of the locomotive is the presence of steps leading to the fuel filler point. Although this batch of shunters was ordered quite early in diesel shunter modernisation terms, they were fitted with electric marker lights from new.*
P. J. Sharpe

The Diesel Shunter

Above: Clearly showing the cab end arrangement is this view of No 11505 at Stratford on 25 May 1956, just three months after delivery. The wheel protection plate below the buffer beam is of quite an unusual design on this class.
Norman Preedy

Below: With obvious signs of renumbering, the original No 11504, by now D2954 is seen at Stratford in December 1960. It is worth noting that this black-liveried example has been given a 'danger overhead live wires' sign on the bodyside, in case it strayed on the Liverpool Street main line.
A. Skinner

The Diesel Shunter

Above: *No 11503, delivered to Stratford on 24 January 1956, is seen outside its home shed on 17 July 1957. In the background is 'large' 0-6-0 No 12135, another resident of the depot. After renumbering to No D2953 the locomotive was eventually withdrawn from Stratford on 19 June 1966 and sold into industrial use at Thames Matex, West Thurrock, after finishing life here it went on to other industrial users in the local area before entering preservation at the now closed South Yorkshire Railway.*
R. K. Evans

Below: *Two members of this class remained in traffic long enough to receive TOPS renumbering, operating on the isolated Holyhead breakwater line in Anglesey. On 23 July 1974 No 01002 is seen at the breakwater quarry. The locomotive still sported black livery but had gained yellow/black warning ends.*
A. M. Clarke

The Diesel Shunter

Ruston & Hornsby 0-4-0 diesel-mechanical 11507-11508 D2957-D2958

This pair of 0-4-0 diesel-mechanical shunting locomotives were ordered under the BTC modernisation plan, aimed at restricted-clearance dock and works terminals, and had a staggeringly small 5ft 9in wheelbase.

The two locomotives, ordered in 1955 from Ruston & Hornsby of Lincoln, were delivered in March and May 1956 and initially operated from Immingham depot being used in the nearby docks. Performance was not good and at the end of 1956 the pair were transferred to Stratford in East London, where after attention at Stratford Works they were were used at various East London dock terminals. The pair remained at Stratford until withdrawal in March 1967 and January 1968 respectively, except for a short period in 1966 when the first of the pair worked at Goole.

When introduced the locomotives carried 1948 'modern traction' numbers 11507 and 11508; under the 1957 BR scheme the two were renumbered to D2957 and D2958. On delivery the locomotives were finished in standard black livery, off-set by a red buffer beam and a Lion over Wheel logo on the cab side above the number.

Air braking was provided for the locomotive, but no train braking was fitted and electric front and rear marker lights were provided from new. An interesting feature of this design was a cast RH (Ruston & Hornsby) plate attached to the front of the raised cab section between the cab windows. This was in addition to the Ruston nameplate on the nose end.

In keeping with all designs of modernisation shunters, removable doors were provided along the bonnet section, to provide access to the power unit and transmission equipment.

After withdrawal by BR, the two locomotives were sold. No D2957 went to Slag Reduction of Ickles, South Yorkshire and was broken up in August 1967. No D2958 was sold to scrap dealer C. F. Booth of Rotherham where it was used as a depot pilot for many years before being broken up in October 1984.

Below: 11507 and 11508 seemed to spend their entire life 'on shed' at Stratford, East London, doing little revenue earning work. However they are recorded as having worked at a number of the East London 'dockland' locations. Sporting its original number 11508 and painted in black livery with Lion on Wheel motif on the cab side, No 11508 is seen at Stratford shed on 11 May 1957, five months after arriving from Immingham. These locomotives were basically a standard Ruston & Hornsby industrial loco, slightly adapted for main line railway company use.
Colin Boocock

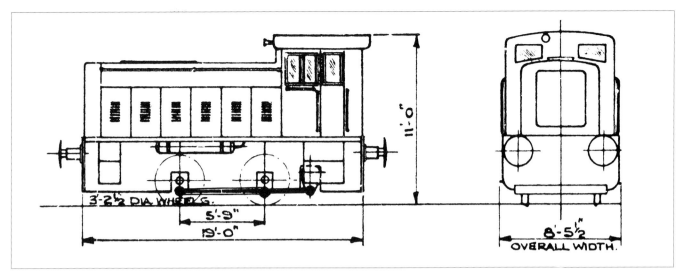

BR 1948 number range:	11507-11508	Power at rail:	117hp
BR 1957 number range:	D2957-D2958	Tractive effort:	14,350lb
Former class code:	DY5, later D1/3 and 1/16	Cylinder bore:	6in
Built by:	Ruston & Hornsby	Cylinder stroke:	5³/4in
Year introduced:	1956	Maximum speed:	15mph
Wheel arrangement:	0-4-0	Brake type:	Air on loco, no train brakes
Weight:	28 tons	Brake force:	15 tons
Height:	11ft 0in	Route availability:	1
Length:	22ft 1³/4in	Heating type:	Not fitted
Width:	8ft 5¹/2in	Multiple coupling type:	Not fitted
Wheelbase:	5ft 9in	Transmission type:	Mechanical — Hunslet 4 speed
Wheel diameter:	3ft 2¹/2in	Fuel tank capacity:	225gal
Min curve negotiable:	1 chain	Cooling water capacity:	15gal
Engine type:	Ruston 6VPHL	Lub oil capacity:	12gal
Engine output:	165hp	Sanding equipment:	Pneumatic

Below: The same locomotive as that in the previous illustration, but now renumbered to D2958 and viewed from the opposite side, the baby Ruston is still basking on shed at Stratford in this 9 August 1959 illustration. This view clearly shows that electric marker lights were fitted from new, but there was no continuous train brake.
A. Swain

The Diesel Shunter

Left: Six removable body side doors were provided on each side of this design to give access to the power unit and transmission. The top part of the bonnet section was also removable (by a workshop), to facilitate major overhaul or rebuild work. No D2958 shows standard black livery in this September 1959 view. K. L. Cook

Below: *This superb broadside illustration of No D2957 shows these small 5ft 9in wheelbase, 19ft long shunters off in all their glory. Again illustrated at Stratford shed, this time on 14 January 1962, this example sports overhead live wire red flashes on the bodyside, as its operating area included London Great Eastern routes which were electrified. A. Swain*

The Diesel Shunter

Ruston & Hornsby 0-6-0 diesel-electric
D2985-D2998
Class 07
07001-07014

Ordered well after the modernisation fleets, was this batch of 14 very handsome 0-6-0 diesel-electric units, designed and built specifically for use within the then massive rail complex at Southampton Docks, which hitherto had used the equally attractive 0-6-0 USA tanks since 1946 when they had been purchased from the War Department.

The locomotives were ordered from Ruston & Hornsby in 1960 and were of slightly unconventional type, with an off-centre cab layout, giving a short (rear) and long (front) nose section. The prime mover, housed in the long nose or bonnet was a Paxman 6RPHL unit of 275hp at 1,360rpm, driving an AEI traction generator group. Output from the generator, powered a single AEI traction motor.

The entire fleet were delivered in 1962 and allocated to the Southern Region shed at Southampton Docks, and by the late 1960s were transferred to the nearby Eastleigh depot.

The 14 strong fleet saw significant use in Southampton Docks, until the complex was run down in terms of wagon load freight, mainly after introduction of the two Dockside Freightliner terminals in the mid-1960s.

Once dock shunting and marshalling work was reduced the fleet commenced operation in the Eastleigh area, working in Eastleigh marshalling yard, the locomotive and vehicle servicing depot and adjacent multiple unit, stock and locomotive works.

When built, the fleet, later identified as Class 07, were fitted with air braking for the locomotive and vacuum train braking, with the more widespread use of air braking, locomotives were modified at Eastleigh Works with dual (air/vacuum) train brakes. A further modification to the braking system was made by fitting a handful of locomotives with high level air brake connections for compatibility with EMU and TC sets, this was used on boat trains to/from Southampton Docks post Bournemouth Line electrification as well as at Eastleigh depot and works.

When introduced the fleet were finished in BR locomotive green, offset by yellow/black chevron ends. A round carriage-type Lion over crown emblem was used on the cab side above the number. After 1967, standard BR blue was applied to repaints, complete with yellow/back warning ends.

Frontal indication was by six electric lights, each capable of showing white or red indication.

Standardisation of traction resources during the 1970s saw the Class 07 fleet slowly phased out, many examples went to industrial users, with only a handful initially being broken up. Several locomotives have subsequently entered preservation.

Right: *A most impressive picture of the first of the Ruston & Hornsby Southern Region 0-6-0 diesel-electric shunters, built expressly for use in Southampton Docks. This view shows the locomotive in the yard of Ruston & Hornsby at Lincoln on 7 May 1962, three weeks prior to delivery to the Southern Region. As can be seen this fleet were delivered in Southern style green livery with a carriage-style Lion over Crown logo. Wasp ends were applied from new.* CJM collection

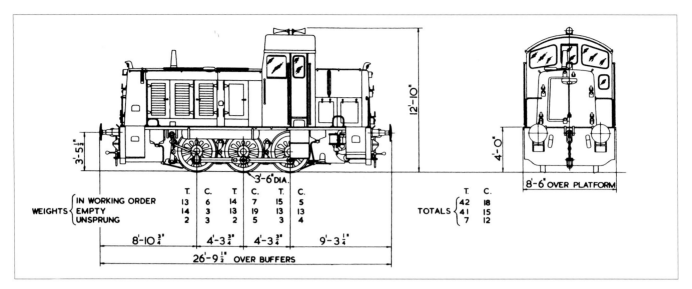

WEIGHTS		T.	C.	T.	C.	T.	C.
	IN WORKING ORDER	13	6	14	7	15	5
	EMPTY	14	3	13	19	13	13
	UNSPRUNG	2	3	2	5	3	3

TOTALS	T.	C.
	42	18
	41	15
	7	12

TOPS number range:	07001-07014
1957 BR number range:	D2985-D2998
Former class code:	2/16
Built by:	Ruston & Hornsby
Year introduced:	1962
Wheel arrangement:	0-6-0
Weight:	43 tons
Height:	12ft 10in
Length:	26ft 9in
Width:	8ft 6in
Wheelbase:	8ft 7$\frac{1}{4}$in
Wheel diameter:	3ft 6in
Min curve negotiable:	2 chains
Engine type:	Paxman 6RPHL MkIII
Engine output:	275hp
Power at rail:	190hp
Tractive effort:	28,800lb
Cylinder bore:	7in
Cylinder stroke:	7$\frac{3}{4}$in
Maximum speed:	20mph
Brake type:	Vacuum, later Dual
Brake force:	36 tons
Route availability:	6
Heating type:	Not fitted
Multiple coupling type:	Not fitted
Main generator type:	AEI RTB 6652
Aux generator type:	AEI
Traction motor type:	AEI RTA 6652
No of traction motors:	1
Fuel tank capacity:	300gal
Cooling water capacity:	26gal
Lub oil capacity:	19$\frac{1}{2}$gal
Sanding equipment:	Pneumatic

Right: *By 1967 when corporate BR rail blue livery was applied, locomotives which went through Eastleigh Works for classified overhaul were repainted in the standard colours. No D2992 is seen in May 1968 at Southampton Eastern Docks, carrying the duty No 7 target on the front end.*
John Bird

Right: *Another of those classic shunter views. Brand new Southern Region 0-6-0 diesel-electric No D2985 stands in the yard at Lincoln prior to shipment south to Southampton. In the background is Lincoln Cathedral. This illustration, perfect for the modellers, shows the locomotive layout in original style. The locomotive is viewed from its main or power unit bonnet section.*
Author's collection

Left: *The Ruston & Hornsby diesel-electric 'dock' shunters were frequently used to pilot or position Ocean Liner boat trains in either the Western or Eastern Docks at Southampton and were often seen passing over the 'town quay' line between the two dock areas. Wearing target '8' No D2997 is seen arriving at the Eastern Docks on 20 May 1967, with stock to form an 'up' Ocean Liner Boat express to Waterloo.* **John Bird**

Right: *Repaints of the class at Eastleigh after March 1967, saw BR standard rail blue applied complete with wasp warning ends. The livery is shown on No D2992, from its short nose end at Southampton Eastern Docks freight yard in May 1968. In the background another blue-liveried classmate can be seen.*
John Bird

Below: *Three of the Southampton Dock shunters pause between duties at the Western Docks on 28 November 1968. The leading locomotive on the right, No 2993 without the 'D' prefix, is a dual brake fitted example complete with high-level air connections.* **John Bird**

The Diesel Shunter

Above: *On its first tour of duty after a classified overhaul at Eastleigh Works, No 2993 is seen in Southampton Docks on 10 October 1968. Several members of this class were overhauled in the mid 1960s and fitted with air brake equipment and high level air pipes in order to haul SR TC stock after detaching from London services at Southampton, through the docks, a method of operation which never in the event took place.*
Colin J. Marsden

Below: *Southampton Docks shed, with three Ruston diesel-electrics on shed. Two are viewed from the No 1 or engine end and the centre locomotive is seen from the control equipment or No 2 end.*
R. Singleton

The Diesel Shunter

Above: *The Ruston diesel-electric shunters were painted from new in BR coaching stock green and carried the coaching stock style roundel on the cab side. No D2986, the second locomotive of the build, is seen at Eastleigh on 21 June 1962.* Author's collection

Left: *This illustration of preserved No D2991, which was allocated the TOPS identity 07007 but was not renumbered, instead being withdrawn in May 1973. This view illustrates the detailed positions of the front end equipment, including six marker lights. This locomotive is vacuum brake fitted only, and is seen at the site of its preservation, Eastleigh Works.*
Colin J. Marsden

Right: *After being withdrawn as surplus to requirements in the Southampton area, mainly due to the change of dock rail traffic, a number of locomotives went into industrial use, with several later entering preservation. No D2994 (07010) at first worked at ICI Billingham and was then preserved on the West Somerset Railway. It is seen here fully restored to green livery at Minehead.*
Colin J. Marsden

The Diesel Shunter

This page: *Three views of the preserved No D2991 at Eastleigh. In the plate above the locomotive is seen in the Works yard shunting one of the rebuilt 1938 stock London Underground tube sets, No 008, on 6 May 1990. This stock was destined for the Isle of Wight to replace 1927 stock. In the view right, the locomotive is seen parked at the side of Eastleigh Works where it was used as a mobile generator for several years from 1973. Its condition was poor, but thankfully this use kept the locomotive in one piece for eventual preservation. In the illustration below, the locomotive is seen outside the BREL Eastleigh Works diesel test house, which was used for many years to evaluate the power output from diesel locomotives and DEMU power cars overhauled at the site.*
All: Colin J. Marsden

The Diesel Shunter

Brush/Beyer Peacock 0-4-0 diesel-electric D2999

As part of a projected second phase of diesel shunter fleets envisaged by the UK rail industry — which of course never materialised, in 1958 the Brush Co of Loughborough and Beyer-Peacock of Manchester entered into a construction partnership to build five 0-4-0 demonstrator locos, fitted with diesel-electric transmission. At the time, it was forseen that BR would be seeking substantial numbers of additional small wheelbase shunting locomotives and the private sector would be keen to explore new developments in industrial locomotive design.

At the time of the partnership, Brush were quickly becoming an established name in main line diesel locomotive construction, with their A1A-A1A Type 2s (later Classes 30 and 31) emerging from the Loughborough factory, however, Beyer Peacock were not having such good fortune, and were still trying to regain the position of superiority they held in the construction of steam traction and rapidly trying to adapt to the new 'modern' rail industry needs. Beyer Peacock saw a partnership with Brush as a favourable way forward.

After construction by Beyer Peacock, the five demonstrators found their way to the Brush Works in Loughborough, being used as workshop pilots, and occasionally finding short term hire contracts with either the nationalised railway or industrial railway users. Although built as demonstrators attempts were made on numerous occasions to sell the 6ft wheelbase locomotives to both the UK mainline and industrial operators; however no buyers were forthcoming.

Although detailed records of the five locomotives are very sketchy, two are known to have operated on the BR network, with one, works number 100, officially entering BR stock as No D2999 albeit for only a short period. The locomotive's history shows that prior to this it had been hired to a quarry in north Kent, where to clear a lineside obstruction the cab had been cut down and was thus identifiable from the other locomotives of the build.

The locomotive's design incorporated a verandah at the cab end, thus providing the cab access via a single door and greatly improving the cab layout. As No D2999, the 0-4-0 machine was used at several locations, mainly in the East London dock areas, where it was allocated to Stratford depot under the control of the Eastern Region. However, the locomotive also operated in the Gloucester Docks.

Although quite surprisingly, the locomotive was eventually sold to BR as No D2999 it was, however, so non-standard that it was deemed as an early candidate for withdrawal under the 1960s National Traction Plan, being withdrawn in 1967 and disposed of in 1970.

When built, the locomotive was finished in workshop grey livery, with the Brush name on the cab side, front and back, after eventual sale to BR, it was re-painted in then standard BR green livery with yellow/black warning ends.

The locomotive was fitted with a 200hp Petter-McLaren LE6 engine which drove a Brush generator group, powering a single Brush traction motor. The locomotive was fitted with air brakes for its own speed reduction, but was not fitted with train brakes.

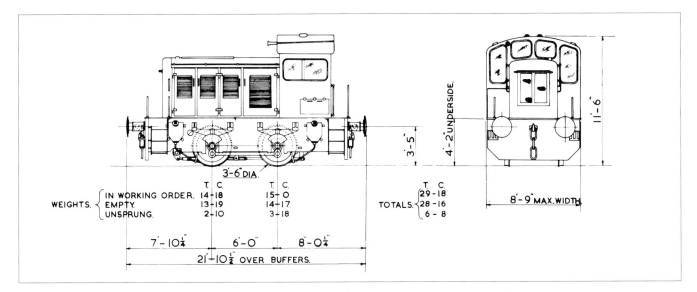

BR 1957 number:	D2999	Wheel diameter:	3ft 6in
Former class code:	D2/11	Min curve negotiable:	1 chain
Built by:	Brush Ltd/Beyer Peacock	Engine type:	National M4 AAV 6
Year built:	1958	Engine output:	200hp
Year introduced to BR:	1960	Power at rail:	152hp
Wheel arrangement:	0-4-0	Tractive effort:	19,200lb
Weight:	30 tons	Cylinder bore:	7in
Height:	11ft 6in	Cylinder stroke:	7^{1}/$_{2}$in
Length:	21ft 10^{1}/$_{2}$in	Maximum speed:	18mph
Width:	8ft 9in	Brake type:	Air on loco, no train brakes
Wheelbase:	6ft 0in	Brake force:	19 tons
		Route availability:	1
		Heating type:	Not fitted
		Multiple coupling type:	Not fitted
		Transmission type:	Electric
		Traction generator:	Brush TG 50-40
		Number of traction motors:	1
		Traction motor type:	Brush TM 50-50 Mk 3
		Fuel tank capacity:	200gal
		Cooling water capacity:	50gal
		Lub oil capacity:	16gal
		Sanding equipment:	Pneumatic

Left: *In Brush Works grey livery, trials locomotive No D2999 is seen at Doncaster Works while being evaluated for use on BR in September 1960. The locomotive is principally an industrial unit adapted for BR use.*
Derek Porter

Below: *By the time this picture was taken at Stratford in 1965, it was painted in BR green and sadly devoid of its Brush works plate.*
F. Hornby

The Diesel Shunter

Brush/Beyer Peacock 0-4-0 diesel-electric D9998

In addition to No D2999, another of the Brush/Beyer Peacock 0-4-0 diesel-electric shunters was sanctioned for use over BR lines. This locomotive was given the identity D9998, with BTC records of the locomotive being very scarce. Records show it arrived on mainline tracks in mid-1961 and was used in Gloucester Docks for around a year before being returned to Brush. The locomotive is reported to have operated without a running number for most of its time on the BR network, but references to the machine in WR minute books refer to it as 'Brush 9998', so whether a 'D' prefix was actually carried or used is in some doubt.

Running number:	D9998 (not always applied)	Tractive effort:	19,200lb
Built by:	Brush Ltd at Beyer Peacock	Maximum speed:	18mph
Year introduced:	1961	Brake type:	Air on loco, no train brakes
Wheel arrangement:	0-4-0	Brake force:	10 tons
Weight:	30 tons	Route availability:	1
Height:	11ft 6in	Heating type:	Not fitted
Length:	21ft 10½in	Multiple coupling type:	Not fitted
Width	8ft 9in	Main generator type:	Brush
Wheelbase:	6ft 0in	Aux generator type :	Brush
Wheel diameter:	3ft 6in	Traction motor type:	Brush
Min curve negotiable:	2 chains	No of traction motors:	1
Engine type:	Petter McLaren	Fuel tank capacity:	200gal
Engine output:	200hp	Lub oil capacity:	16gal
Power at rail:	160hp	Sanding equipment:	Pneumatic

Below: *The second of the Brush prototype 0-4-0 'small' dock shunters to be authorised for use over BR lines was given the identity of D9998. Without running number, the locomotive is seen shunting freight stock at Gloucester Docks on 4 October 1962.* **B. J. Ashworth**

Brush Industrial 0-4-0s

This page: *Although these locomotives were not authorised to operate on the UK national railway network, they represent the major contribution Brush Traction made in supplying small industrial shunting locos. The company tried several times to enter the mainstream shunting locomotive market but sadly failed. In industrial terms their products have always been highly reliable and well accepted by operators. The locomotive above is Works No 3096 of 1956 and is a full width cab 0-4-0. The illustration below shows another of the mid-1950s built 300hp machines, Works No 3100 which was used by the National Coal Board to replace steam traction. Records show the livery was light grey.*
Both: Author's collection

BR Workshops 0-6-0 diesel-electric
13000-13366, D3000-D4192
Class 08, 09, 10, unclassified
08001-08995, 09001-09026,
09101-09107, 09201-09205

The word 'standard' in relation to UK modern traction locomotives can rarely be used, but the 1950s-ordered large 350hp diesel-electric shunters most certainly come under this title, with a total of 1,193 locomotives of like design built over a 10-year period from 1952.

UK's standard diesel shunting locomotive is a direct development of the 1944-built LMS/EE design, with a few detail differences, such as 4ft 6in diameter wheels to suit general operating conditions and slight body changes allowing the fleet to meet the then L1 gauge profile, permitting virtually unrestricted access to the rail network, except for routes barred by axle-load restrictions.

The first batch of 'standard' 350hp DE shunters were ordered from BR workshops in the early 1950s, with construction of the first tranche awarded to Derby Works, from where the first locomotive, numbered 13000, emerged on 11 October 1952. After immediate on works trials, the locomotive went to Toton for proving tests before being shipped to the Western Region for service deployment.

Following the initial order for Derby Works, such was the speed in which the BTC wanted to modernise the shunting operations of the rail network, displacing steam, that subsequent orders were placed with Derby, Crewe, Darlington, Doncaster and Horwich works.

The standard prime mover adopted was the time proven English Electric 6K of 350hp, coupled to an English Electric generator set. However during the build process it was decided to experiment with other power unit/generator pairings (as detailed in the class tables), however none proved as satisfactory as the 6K/EE pairing which was the standard design.

In terms of body design, all locomotives were the same, measuring 29ft 3in in length, with a cab at one end and a nose or bonnet section housing the engine, generator and control equipment. The radiator was at the nose end. The power unit and other equipment was accessed by removable hinged side doors and roof sections. The driving cab offered restricted visibility in the direction of the bonnet but this was accepted by the drivers of the day who were used to handling steam traction with a smoky boiler protruding in the front direction of travel.

Directly in front of the cab section were frame mounted fuel tanks, with saddle boxes mounted on the frame housing batteries, vacuum exhauster and later an air compressor. On initial delivery all locomotives were fitted with vacuum brakes, but as the build progressed a number were assembled with the provision of dual (vacuum/air) braking.

The body ends were fitted with electric marker lights, which could have a red shade slid over to provide a tail indication.

363 locomotives were built carrying the 1948 series five digit 13xxx running numbers, before the 1957 D3xxx and D4xxx series were introduced. Early built locomotives emerged painted in all over black livery, this was replaced by BR locomotive green from the late 1950s. Wasp yellow/black warning ends were progressively applied.

During the course of the build, batches totalling 26 locomotives destined for use by the Southern Region were fitted with a revised gear ratio, allowing a maximum speed of 27½mph, more in keeping with trip working over the congested south of England network.

From 1966/7 standard rail blue was applied as the basic colour scheme, off-set by white BR logo and running numbers. Under the numeric classification system the standard locomotives became Class 08, while those with the higher maximum speed became Class 09. Class 10 was allocated to the batches of locomotives fitted with a Blackstone power unit and GEC supplied generator. When the TOPS renumbering system was introduced from 1973 only locomotives of Class 08 and 09 remained, the Class 10 fleet having been withdrawn as non-standard.

A large number of modifications and changes have befallen this huge class over the years, these are largely detailed in the following illustrations. However some are worthy of more detailed explanation. Two batches of Class 08s have been modified over the years as Class 08/9s for working over the restricted height gauge BPGV line in West Wales.

In 1992-93 a batch of 12 standard Class 08s were rebuilt by RFS Engineering at Kilnhurst as Class 09, being fitted with modified gearing. The locomotives were re-classified 09/1 and 09/2 reflecting whether they were fitted with 110V or 90V auxiliary electrics.

Although at the time of the mid-1990s privatisation of the UK railways around 500 standard design shunters remained in service, their operation was much reduced. The fleet was divided among the principal operators, with the freight companies obviously taking the lions share. Refurbishment of the fleet is now under way, with EWS effecting a modernisation programme to make these 50 year old locomotives suitable for a few more years work. At present no plans are on the cards to replace these stalwart workhorses, except by using more train locomotives to perform shunting operations. However there are still many cases where the use of a dedicated shunting locomotive is deemed as required.

Six locomotives are also worth special note, which were rebuilt in 1965 to form three high-adhesion master and slave units for use in Tinsley marshalling yard, these are covered in a separate chapter on page 204.

Upon completion of their useful life for the mainstream railway, a large number of standard 0-6-0s passed into industrial use; many have been exported for overseas use, while others have worked for numerous UK private operators.

In more recent years, a considerable number of locomotives have gone into preservation, where their switch-on and go capability has been very useful.

Since the privatisation of UK railways, the private owner hire operators have come to the fore, where businesses such as Cotswold Rail, RT Rail, Wabtec and HNRC have purchased fleets of shunters, refurbished them and then offered them for re-hire to the mainstream railway operators.

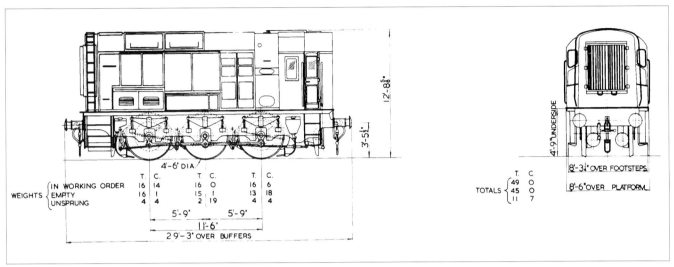

Below: Representing the UK's largest ever fleet of modern traction locos, the standard BTC/BR 0-6-0 diesel-electric shunter is No 13005, painted in BTC black livery and viewed from its left side. This locomotive was built at BR Derby Works and entered traffic on 21 November 1952 at Ayr in south-west Scotland. It was renumbered to D3005 in September 1958 and again to 08002 in March 1974, finally being withdrawn in September 1977.
Author's collection

Sub class:	08/0	08/9
TOPS number range:	08001-08958	08991-08995
Original 1948 number range:	13000-13366	-
1957 BR number range:	D3000-D4192	-
Former class codes:	DEJ4, then D3/2, 3/1	08/0
Built by:	BR workshops Derby, Crewe, Darlington, Doncaster, Horwich	BR Landore
Years introduced:	1953-59	1985-87
Wheel arrangement:	0-6-0	0-6-0
Weight:	48-49 tons	48-49 tons
Height:	12ft 8⅝in	11ft 10in
Length:	29ft 3in	29ft 3in
Width :	8ft 6in	8ft 6in
Wheelbase:	11ft 6in	11ft 6in
Wheel diameter:	4ft 6in	4ft 6in
Min curve negotiable:	3 chains	3 chains
Engine type:	English Electric 6KT	English Electric 6KT
Engine output:	400hp	400hp
Power at rail:	260hp	260hp
Tractive effort:	35,000lb	35,000lb
Cylinder bore:	10in	10in
Cylinder stroke:	12in	12in
Maximum speed:	15-20mph	15-20mph
Brake type:	Originally vacuum, some modified to dual and others to air only	Dual
Brake force:	19 tons	19 tons
Route availability:	5	5
Heating type:	Not fitted	Not fitted
Multiple coupling type:	Not fitted	Not fitted
Main generator type:	EE801-8E or E801-14E	EE801-8E or E801-14E
Aux generator type:	90V locos - EE736-2D or EE736-4E 110V locos - EE906-3D	EE736-2D or EE736-4E
Traction motor type:	EE506-6A or EE506-7C	EE506-6A
No of traction motors:	2	2
Gear ratio:	Overall - 23.9:1 First train - 82:15 Second train - 70:16	Overall - 23.9:1 First train - 82:15 Second train - 70:16
Fuel tank capacity:	668gal	668gal
Lub oil capacity:	45gal	45gal
Cooling water capacity:	140gal	140gal
Sanding equipment:	Pneumatic	Pneumatic
Special fittings:	Some locos - Radio	Some locos - Radio

Sub-class variations

08/0 — Standard locomotive used for yard shunting and pilot duties, a direct descendant of LMS prewar design
08/9 — Locomotives modified from Class 08/0 with reduced cab height for use on BPGV line in West Wales

Special features

08765/841/901 — Waterproofed for use at Oxley carriage washing plant.
08480/571/588/641/643-645/651/745/888/908 — Fitted with buck-eye couplings.
08414 — Fitted with siren and flashing light for working at Ipswich docks.
08948 — Fitted with Scharfenberg couplings for shunting Eurostars.
08866/921 — Fitted with remote control equipment, supplied by Cattron Systems and Hima Sella Systems respectively.
Some locomotives have high-level air pipes.

Above: *A view inside the main erecting shop at BR Darlington Works on 3 September 1957 shows No D3439, one of the Blackstone engine-fitted GEC-equipped locomotives under assembly. It can clearly be seen from the locomotive in the rear that the power unit was placed on the frame at an early stage of assembly and the body frame built around. In the foreground are the three wheelsets for No D3439, the two outer sets complete with traction motors, awaiting fitting. This locomotive emerged on 29 September 1957 and was allocated to King's Cross.* **Author's collection**

Right: *The 'standard' shunter assembly work at BR Derby Works was mainly carried out in two roads of the main erecting shop, with around 15 locomotives under assembly at one time. This January 1960 view shows No D3942 in advance stages of assembly. This locomotive was delivered to Percy Main shed on the North Eastern Region on 26 March 1960. The locomotive was later renumbered to 08774 and is now in traffic with A. V. Dawson of Middlesbrough.* **Author's collection**

The Diesel Shunter

Sub class:	09/0	09/1	09/2
TOPS number range:	09001-09026	09101-09107	09201-09205
1957 number range:	D3665-71, D3719-21, D4099-D4114	Rebuilt from Class 08	Rebuilt from Class 08
Former class codes:	DEJ4, then 3/1	Rebuilt from Class 08	Rebuilt from Class 08
Built by:	BR workshops - Darlington and Horwich	RFS Kilnhurst	RFS Kilnhurst
Years introduced:	1959-62	1992-93	1992-93
Wheel arrangement:	0-6-0	0-6-0	0-6-0
Weight:	49 tons	49 tons	49 tons
Height:	12ft 8⅝in	12ft 8⅝in	12ft 8⅝in
Length:	29ft 3in	29ft 3in	29ft 3in
Width:	8ft 6in	8ft 6in	8ft 6in
Wheelbase:	11ft 6in	11ft 6in	11ft 6in
Wheel diameter:	4ft 6in	4ft 6in	4ft 6in
Min curve negotiable:	3 chains	3 chains	3 chains
Engine type:	English Electric 6KT	English Electric 6KT	English Electric 6KT
Engine output:	400hp	400hp	400hp
Power at rail:	269hp	269hp	269hp
Tractive effort:	25,000lb	25,000lb	25,000lb
Cylinder bore:	10in	10in	10in
Cylinder stroke:	12in	12in	12in
Maximum speed:	27½mph	27½mph	27½mph
Brake type:	Dual	Dual	Dual
Brake force:	19 tons	19 tons	19 tons
Route availability:	5	5	5
Heating type:	Not fitted	Not fitted	Not fitted
Multiple coupling type:	Not fitted	Not fitted	Not fitted
Main generator type:	EE801-13E or EE801-14E	EE801-13E or EE801-14E	EE801-13E or EE801-14E
Aux generator type:	EE906-3D	EE906-3D	EE906-3D
Traction motor type:	EE506-10C	EE506-10C	EE506-10C
No of traction motors:	2	2	2
Gear ratio:	Overall - 23.9:1 First train - 82:15 Second train - 70:16	Overall - 23.9:1 First train - 82:15 Second train - 70:16	Overall - 23.9:1 First train - 82:15 Second train - 70:16
Fuel tank capacity:	668gal	668gal	668gal
Lub oil capacity:	45gal	45gal	45gal
Cooling water capacity:	140gal	140gal	140gal
Sanding equipment:	Pneumatic	Pneumatic	Pneumatic

Sub class variations

Class 09/0

Higher-speed version of standard 0-6-0 shunter (Class 08) originally allocated to the former BR Southern Region.

Class 09/1

Modified from standard Class 08, fitted with 110V electrical equipment.

Class 09/2

Modified from standard Class 08, fitted with original 90V electrical equipment.

Note

Many ex-Southern Region locomotives are fitted with dual high level air/main reservoir pipes.

Right: *General view of part of the Darlington assembly shop for BR 'standard' 0-6-0 diesel-electric locos. On the left is a near-complete loco, while on the right is a frame unit awaiting the installation of a prime mover, before the cab section, radiator compartment and body frame were added. Records from Darlington show that assembly from sheet steel to an operational locomotive took around 12 weeks.*
Author's collection

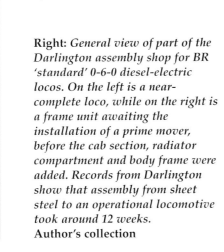

BR 1948 number range:	13137-13151
BR 1957 number range:	D3137-D3151, D3439-D3453, D3473-D3502, D3612-D3651, D4049-D4094
TOPS classification:	10
Former class codes:	DEJ 5, later D3/4, 3/1C
Built by:	BR Darlington, BR Doncaster
Years introduced:	1955-1962
Wheel arrangement:	0-6-0
Weight:	49 tons
Height:	12ft 8 $^5/_8$in
Length:	29ft 3in
Width :	8ft 6in
Wheelbase:	11ft 6in
Wheel diameter:	4ft 6in
Min curve negotiable:	3 chains
Engine type:	Blackstone ER6
Engine output:	350hp
Power at rail:	194hp
Tractive effort:	35,000lb
Cylinder bore:	9in
Cylinder stroke:	11in
Maximum speed:	15mph
Brake type:	Air on loco, vacuum on train
Brake force:	19 tonnes
Route availability:	5
Heating type:	Not fitted
Multiple coupling type:	Not fitted
Main generator type:	GEC
Aux generator type :	GEC
Traction motor type:	GEC
No of traction motors:	2
Gear ratio:	§
Fuel tank capacity:	668gal
Lub oil capacity:	45gal
Cooling water capacity:	140gal
Sanding equipment:	Pneumatic

Above: *Another view of the Blackstone/GEC assembly line at Darlington Works. The frame with its power unit and generator nearest the camera is locomotive No D3445, a loco which was handed over on 21 October 1957 to New England shed, Peterborough.* **Author's collection**

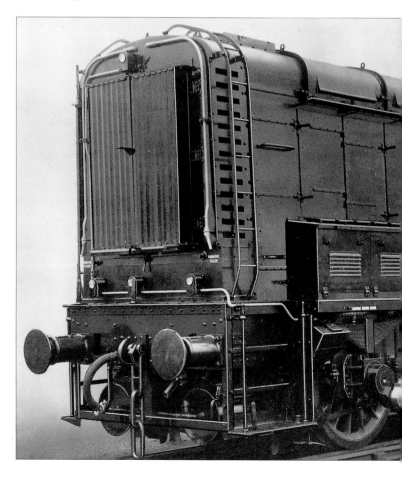

The Diesel Shunter

Above: The 10 Crossley engine, Crompton Parkinson equipped 'standard' 0-6-0s were numbered 13117-126 when released from the BR workshops Derby between June 1955 and June 1957, their protracted delivery being caused by a supply shortage of components and less than satisfactory performance. As with all 'new builds' an official picture was taken of the first off the production line. In reality the external appearance was no different from any other of the fleet. No 13117, like all members of the build, was shedded at Toton depot.
Author's collection

Below: No 13152, built at Darlington in February 1955 was the first of 15 locomotives fitted with a Blackstone engine driving BTH electrical equipment. The official picture is very slightly 'touched-up' by the BTH photographic unit to show the finer detail of the bodywork. This locomotive was allocated to Immingham depot. Due to its non-standard power and control equipment it had a relatively short life and was withdrawn for scrap in September 1967. No 13152 was renumbered to D3152 on 13 February 1960.
Author's collection

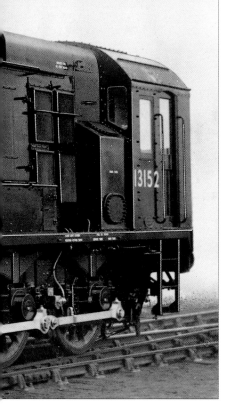

BR 1948 number range:	13117-13126	13152-13166
BR 1957 number range:	D3117-D3126	D3152-D3166
Former class code:	D3/3, later 3/1B	DEJ6, later D3/5, 3/1D
Built by:	BR Derby	BR Darlington
Year built:	1955	1955
Wheel arrangement:	0-6-0	0-6-0
Weight:	48 tons	48 tons
Height:	12ft 8⁵/8in	12ft 8⁵/8in
Length:	29ft 3in	29ft 3in
Width:	8ft 6in	8ft 6in
Wheelbase:	11ft 6in	11ft 6in
Wheel diameter:	4ft 6in	4ft 6in
Min curve negotiable:	3 chains	3 chains
Engine type:	Crossley ESNT6	Blackstone ER6T
Engine output:	350hp	350hp
Power at rail:	194hp	194hp
Tractive effort:	35,000lb	35,000lb
Cylinder bore:	10in	10in
Cylinder stroke:	12in	12in
Maximum speed:	20mph	20mph
Brake type:	Air on loco, vacuum train brakes	Air on loco, vacuum train brakes
Brake force:	19 tonnes	19 tonnes
Route availability:	5	5
Heating type:	Not fitted	Not fitted
Multiple coupling type:	Not fitted	Not fitted
Transmission type:	Electric	Electric
Main generator:	Crompton Parkinson	BTH
Aux generator:	Crompton Parkinson	BTH
Number of traction motors:	2	2
Traction motor type:	Crompton Parkinson	BTH
Fuel tank capacity:	668gal	668gal
Lub oil capacity:	45gal	45gal
Cooling water capacity:	140gal	140gal
Sanding equipment:	Pneumatic	Pneumatic

The Diesel Shunter

Above: *Carrying BR black livery, No 13238 is seen at Hull Neptune Street on 11 April 1956 performing yard pilot duties. This locomotive was at the time allocated to York depot. It was later renumbered D3238 and eventually 08170. It was finally withdrawn in March 1986.* Author's collection

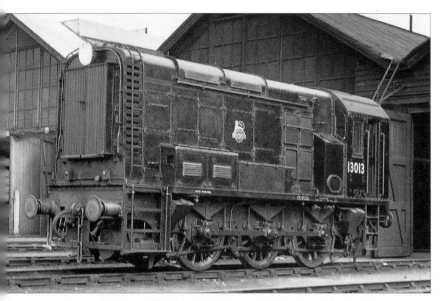

Above: *With a tell-tale white disc on the front end, indicating Southern Region, No 13013 is seen 'on shed' at Eastleigh. This locomotive was built at Derby in December 1952 and had just a 20-year life, working exclusively on the Southern.* Brian Morrison

Left: *Painted in standard black livery with a red buffer beam No 13101 is seen at Derby on 4 February 1955 when brand new awaiting transfer to the Southern Region at Norwood Junction. This locomotive remained on the Southern until withdrawn in May 1972 and sold to ARC and used at Loughborough aggregate sidings. When its useful life was over, No 3101, as it was numbered by then, was sold to the Great Central Railway Preservation Society.* Author's collection

The Diesel Shunter

Below: Carrying Crewe 'target' number 16, 'standard' 0-6-0 No 13050 is seen when new shunting a rake of wooden coal wagons at Crewe Sorting Sidings, South. This locomotive entered traffic at Crewe in May 1954 and transferred south to Willesden just six months later. **Author's collection**

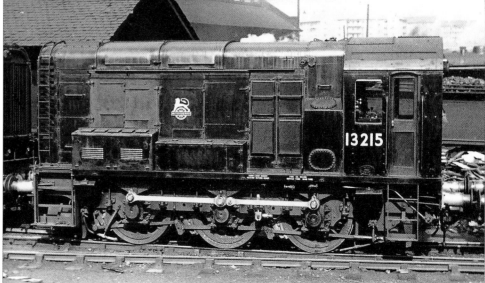

Right: One of the problems of such a 'standard' fleet as this massive build, was that every area of the country quickly had locomotives of identical shape, colour and performance. Initially very few regional or area differences were to be found on the fleet. Here No 13215 is seen at St Rollox, Glasgow on 22 April 1957. This locomotive was delivered in March 1956 and remained in Scotland and the North East all its working life, being withdrawn in July 1983. **R. E. Vincent**

The Diesel Shunter

Above: *With two electrification vehicles coupled to its nose end, No 13176 is seen from its cab end during West Coast electrification work in 1961 between Crewe and Liverpool.* Author's collection

Right: *Tinsley allocated No 13333 is seen in Wath Yard on 7 May 1957. This locomotive was built at Darlington the previous January.* B. K. Green

Below: *This view near Hull Dairycoats, was taken on 21 May 1956 and shows No 13081 powering a local trip working.* Author's collection

Above: *Traversing the Tilmanstone Colliery branch in East Kent, black-liveried No D3044 powers a coal train out of Golgotha Tunnel in April 1960. This locomotive was delivered on 17 March 1954 to Norwood Junction and after withdrawal from BR in 1974 was sold to Foster Yeoman of Merehead Quarry, where it became No 33* **Mendip.**
Derek Cross

This view of Truro in Cornwall is hardly recognisable today, with only a couple of sidings left in the once-busy yard. In this October 1958 view, all-over green-liveried No D3510, complete with ex-GW shunting truck and a short rake of wagons including a horse box set back out of the yard to make a shunting move. No D3510 was allocated new to Plymouth Laira in May 1958 and was a frequent visitor to the Duchy for many years.
B. A. Butt

Left: *One of the sizeable batch of 0-6-0s built by Crewe Works was No D3737. This locomotive emerged in May 1959 for the Scottish Region and allocated to Dalry Road. The livery shown is standard BR locomotive green, with the standard British Railways logo on the battery box. The buffer beams were finished in red, as were the connecting rods. This locomotive was later renumbered to 08570.*
P. J. Sharpe

Right: *Where a number of workshops were building the 'large' 0-6-0s concurrently, locomotives from various batches were entering traffic at the same time. With a small 'D' prefix to its number. No D3609, a Horwich-built locomotive is seen at Doncaster in April 1958 while on delivery from Horwich to Stratford. This example is painted in standard locomotive green, but has the British Railways logo on the engine room side doors.*
R. K. Evans

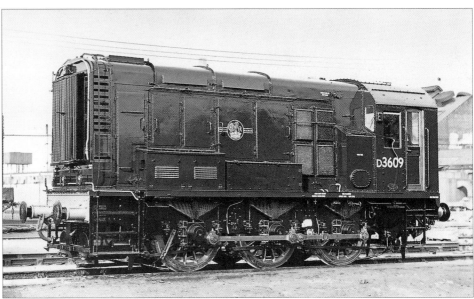

Above: *Another locomotive with a small 'D' prefix to its number is D3478, one of the Darlington Works-built Blackstone/GEC locos. No D3478 emerged in January 1958, just three months before D3609 above, and was allocated to Hatfield; it is seen here awaiting transfer from Darlington when new. The non-standard nature of the Blackstone fitted locomotives saw them only in service for a short period, this locomotive being withdrawn after just 10 years and six months in traffic.*
A. W. Martin

The Diesel Shunter

Above: *Many sighting trials were conducted on 'standard' 0-6-0 shunting locomotives before the form of warning end to be adopted was agreed. In August 1958, trials commenced with a pair of Doncaster built locos, Nos D3682 and D3683. The radiator end paint experiment of No D3683 is shown here, consisting of a yellow surround, with just the lower section of the grille painted in wasp style. The locomotive's livery is BR locomotive green, with a red buffer beam.*
Derek Porter

Right: *The cab warning end was also just applied to the lower section, with the area above waist height painted in standard BR green. After a short period the decision was taken to adopt full wasp markings on both end. When this picture was taken at Stratford on 7 September 1958, the nose end had been modified with wrap round yellow/black wasp bands.*
A. Swain

Left: Close up view of Doncaster-built No D3683 inside the main erecting shop at Doncaster in August 1958. In addition to the trial wasp end, the radiator water filler pipes were also finished in the latest BR standard colour of blue. D. G. Myers

Below: Rounding the curve off the Govan branch at Ibrox station, Glasgow, No D3200 powered a short engineers train. The platforms on the left, by the signal box, are those Glasgow Rangers football trains once served, in the days when large numbers of football specials operated. Author's collection

Below: With the BR Lion over Crown logo facing the cab rather than the radiator end, No D4093 one of the Blackstone/GEC locos, allocated Class 10 under TOPS, is seen at Darlington soon after completion in June 1962. By the time this illustration had been taken, cab doors were finished in steel rather than wood and some minor refinements to construction had been introduced. No D4093 was allocated from new to Tinsley, Sheffield and remained in traffic only until August 1968. P. J. Sharpe

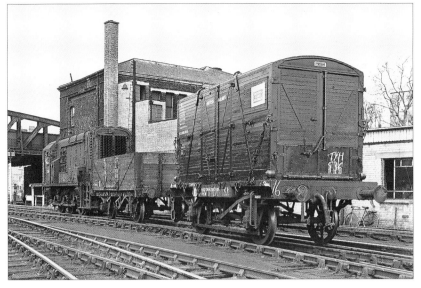

Right: *Loose shunting is seen in operation at Camden Yard, North London, in the summer of 1966. The locomotive used is Willesden-allocated No D3847. This locomotive eventually became No 08680 and was withdrawn from Eastfield in 1992. The wagon nearest the camera is a container mounted on a flat wagon, note the road vehicle registration number scrawled on the container end.*
Author's collection

Left: *During the course of London Midland Region mid-1960s electrification work, the 'standard' 0-6-0 shunter fleet was frequently deployed on overhead electrification erection trains. Here No D3870, sporting BR green livery with full wasp ends is seen near Speke, Liverpool.*
Author's collection

Right: *Sporting full BR rail blue livery, white numbers and white BR logo on the body side, No 08889 is seen at Doncaster after release from the nearby BREL works from a classified overhaul in March 1975. This locomotive had also received dual brake (air/vacuum) equipment during its overhaul, enabling the locomotive to efficiently operate modern stock. At the time of this illustration No 08889 was allocated to Shirebrook.*
Norman Preedy

Left: *Showing distinct signs of a local renumbering from the 'D' series, No 08140 is seen at Gloucester Horton Road depot on 22 August 1974. This locomotive had also received a non-standard BR double arrow logo on the battery box side panel. This locomotive is a vacuum braked only example.*
Norman Preedy

The Diesel Shunter

Right: *Classified overhauls to the 'standard' 0-6-0 shunting fleet were undertaken at around 10 year intervals, or dependent on physical conditions, and miles operated. here No 08606 is seen being re-united with an overhauled set of wheels at Swindon Works in June 1974. Lifting of the locomotive was achieved by inserting a lifting lug into a cut-out in the buffer beam, and attaching this via chains to an overhead crane.*
Colin J. Marsden

Below: *Until the abolition of much of the parcels train network, Class 08 type shunters could be found at most main stations. Here No 08802 is seen at Newcastle, stabled in one of the south bays with a BG on 22 January 1990. This locomotive sports dual air and vacuum brake equipment and had been modified to have only two dual red/white marker/tail lights, one above each buffer.*
Colin J. Marsden

Above: *The shunter fleet was often seen as nocturnal, with a considerable amount of their station work carried out at night after passenger services had ceased. Not a location one would immediately associate with Class 08s is Paddington, but frequently in the days of newspaper trains a locomotive was to be found shunting van stock in the terminus. On 17 October 1984, No 08944 is seen with three vans in platform 10.*
Colin J. Marsden

Below and Below Right: *In the 1980s and 1990s a number of depots applied local additions to many main line and shunting locos, to personalise individual locos. Tinsley applied a slight livery variation to No 08691, which gained a yellow painted sole bar, its running number on the battery box and an oversize BR logo on the cab side. These two illustrations show the locomotive performing station pilot duties at Sheffield Midland station on 13 February 1991.*
Colin J. Marsden

The Diesel Shunter

Above: *For many years the up Travelling Post Office train from Penzance to Paddington used to attach an additional mail van at Exeter St Davids. This was frequently done by the yard Class 08, which positioned the van in platform No 6 to await the arrival of the mail train in platform 5, then attaching the van on the rear of the set. On 14 July 1983 No 08954 awaits the shunt signal to pull out the station and onto Exe Bridge, while Class 33 No 33019 awaits its next turn of duty on the Waterloo line in the shed.*
Colin J. Marsden

The Diesel Shunter

Left: Allerton depot near Liverpool, built as part of the 1960s electrification of the London Midland, became the home of many 0-6-0 shunting locomotives in the 1990s, frequently with locomotives receiving heavy repairs at the depot. In this view taken on 10 March 1993, four locomotives, Nos 08856, 08902, 08913 and 08485 await their next tours of duty. No 08856, nearest the camera, is a dual brake example, identified by the presence of two main reservoir pipes and an air brake pipe on the buffer beam.
Colin J. Marsden

Right: For many years the principal depot for maintaining shunter motive power for use in the London area of the Southern Region was Selhurst. Here a mix of standard Class 08 and higher-speed Class 09/0s could be found. No 09012, named **Dick Hardy**, is seen inside the 'new' running shed at the depot on 4 September 1991. This locomotive sports additional high level air pipes, allowing coupling with Southern Region waist height brake pipe fitted EMU and DMU stock.
Colin J. Marsden

Left: For use in the Manchester area, a one-off livery was applied to No 08721 in the late 1980s, in support of the railways parcels and Red Star business. The locomotive was also unofficially named **Starlet**. Painted in BR rail blue with a red band and additional decals, No 08721 is seen inside Longsight depot on 27 February 1990 in company with No 08624 painted in conventional BR rail blue.
Colin J. Marsden

The Diesel Shunter

Above: *The RFS workshops at Kilnhurst near Doncaster undertook a number of classified overhauls on Class 08s and conversions to Class 09/1 and 09/2 in the early 1990s. These were some of the first private engineering overhauls undertaken on the 'standard' shunter fleet. On 11 May 1990, Nos 08757 (left) and 08170 (right) are seen at the Kilnhurst facility.*
Colin J. Marsden

Below: *Newport Ebbw Junction depot was always a home for a batch of Class 08s operating in the sizeable yards and steel complex in the South Wales area. Looking down at the long closed and demolished shed on 14 July 1980, No 08594 is seen in company with a Class 120 DMMU and a Class 37.*
Colin J. Marsden

The Diesel Shunter

Above: *Selhurst repair shop was responsible, along with Eastleigh Works, for carrying out classified overhauls to Southern Region-allocated Class 08 and 09 locos. Here dual brake, high-level pipe fitted No 08648 is seen on blocks while undergoing a wheelset change in June 1979.*
Colin J. Marsden

Above: *Another view taken inside Selhurst repair shop, shows No 09005 parked over the inspection pit, while a Class 455 EMU sits behind. This Class 09 has had its mid-height marker lights plated over, rather than removed.*
Colin J. Marsden

Left: *After the decision was taken to concentrate on air braking for all rolling stock, the need to maintain operational vacuum brake equipment on the shunter fleet reduced and in many cases by the 1990s the redundant equipment was removed. Here lined green-liveried No 08793 and InterCity-liveried No 08570 share depot space with two BR rail blue locomotives at Haymarket, Edinburgh on 29 April 1990.*
Colin J. Marsden

The Diesel Shunter

Above: *The Liverpool Street Station Pilot was always a celebrity locomotive on the Great Eastern. In steam days the locomotive was always kept in immaculate condition and in the 1990s the Class 08 allocated to the work, No 08833 was repainted by Stratford in GE blue. The locomotive is seen inside the DRS at Stratford with Class 86 No 86217 on 26 March 1991, the day of official closure of the heavy repair facility.*
Colin J. Marsden

Right: *Another of the depot local brandings was the application of depot logos on some fleets. Thornaby depot adopted the Kingfisher, seen applied to No 08817, a locomotive also unofficially named* Thornaby. *Illustrated at Darlington on 1 May 1986.*
Colin J. Marsden

The Diesel Shunter

Above: *The make up of the Royal Mail trains at Plymouth was the preserve of a Class 08 or 09 shunter for many years, but today this work is performed by train locos. On 12 March 1990 No 08801 pushes back a rake of Royal Mail stock into one of the bay platforms.*
Colin J Marsden

Left: *Clapham Junction yard operated two Class 09 (or occasionally a Class 08) as pilot for many years up until the early 1990s. Their work consisted of reforming and shunting locomotive hauled stock for the South West services used on the Waterloo-Exeter line as well as boat trains for Southampton and Weymouth. On 5 March 1981 Nos 09015 and 09017 pause between duties.*
Colin J. Marsden

Below: *With the shunter climbing aboard, rail blue-liveried No 08791 hauls a rake of MGR hoppers out of Newport Docks towards Ebbw Junction on 14 July 1980.*
Colin J. Marsden

Above: *The massive yards at Healey Mills near Wakefield were once a hive of activity. On 8 December 1981 No 08706 prepares to 'fiddle shunt' a string of wagons.*
Colin J. Marsden

Below: *With a rake of HTV household coal wagons behind, Ayr-allocated No 08448 pilots a rake of loaded coal out of Ayr Harbour on 12 April 1985. Since construction this locomotive has received simplification of the cab end lights with just the three at buffer beam level retained. For some reason this dual brake-fitted example at the time of this picture had its vacuum pipe removed and its air pipes tied up in a knot.*
Colin J. Marsden

The Diesel Shunter

Above: *Most general freight traffic in the Plymouth area has been dealt with at Tavistock Junction yard for many years, which still today retains a rostered 'pilot' locomotive. On 25 June 1981, No 08377 performs shunting operations, while Class 37 No 37142 awaits to work a clay train to the west.*
Colin J. Marsden

Right: *Air brake only fitted, BR rail blue-liveried No 08703 stands in the Ince & Elton line platform at Helsby on 15 September 1992 with a single fertiliser wagon from the now-closed Ince Marshes Kemira sidings.*
Colin J. Marsden

The Diesel Shunter

Above: *Dual brake-fitted blue-liveried No 08904 shunts a rake of Mk 1 sleeper stock in Willesden carriage sidings on 12 May 1980.*
Colin J. Marsden

Left: *Complete with RPPR headboard, No 08274 shunt releases a railtour in the steelworks at Consett on 12 May 1979. It is unlikely that today such freedom would be given to railtour passengers to roam and photograph the train.*
Colin J. Marsden

Below: *High-level air-brake fitted No 08653 stands at the head of an engineers train at London Bridge station on 13 June 1978 during station rebuilding work.*
Colin J. Marsden

The Diesel Shunter

Above: *It has never been common to see Class 08s powering main line trains! However on some rare occasions fleet members have been used to rescue failed services. On 1 June 1985 No 08591 is seen propelling No 47461 into Ayr carriage sidings following a failure before departure of the 07.45 Ayr-Euston 'Royal Scot'.*
Alan Sherratt

Below: *Some of the Southern Region Class 09s were fitted with additional cab end marker lights, as shown here on No 09002 at Woking on 15 May 1981. This locomotive has two additional lights below the cab windows. No 09002 after withdrawal was sold to the Devon Diesel Society and is preserved at Buckfastleigh.*
Colin J. Marsden

The Diesel Shunter

Left: *A small batch of air brake-fitted Class 08s was modified in the mid-1980s with drop-head knuckle couplers to attach to HST trailer stock. The simple modification saved many problems in attachment of conventional couplings to the fixed auto couplers of the HSTs. No 08480 is seen at Old Oak Common with its HST coupling in the raised position. This is one of many locomotives which passed through works for classified overhaul in the late 1970s and early 1980s and had its vacuum brake equipment removed.*
Colin J. Marsden

Right: *A fascinating modification was made to West Midlands-based No 08841 in the late 1980s, that of fitting a rubber skirt on the sides of the running plate to stop the ingress of water into the running gear when passing through the coach washer at Oxley, Wolverhampton. The locomotive, painted in standard rail blue, is seen at Wolverhampton on 14 September 1988.*
Steve Widdowson

Left: *As part of the retention of the important corporate image, perhaps too much freedom was allowed by local depots in the 1980s and 1990s, as many rather non-standard livery modifications were to be found. These hideous livery modifications were carried out by staff at Fratton near Portsmouth to No 09025 and included Network SouthEast branding, silver wheels and sand boxes and the painted name Victory on the roof panel. One could hardly imagine that such alterations to the BR image would have been allowed in the 1950s!*
Thomas Silsbury

The Diesel Shunter

Right: *Mishaps have always occurred to rolling stock and locomotives and even in the best controlled circles problems do occur. No 08948, shown here at Old Oak Common on 22 February 1984, sustained this damage while shunting at Acton yard when it collided with parked wagons. This locomotive was later rebuilt by Swindon works, and went on to become the selected Class 08 to be modified for use at North Pole Eurostar depot being fitted with drop head Scharfenburg couplers.*
Colin J. Marsden

Left: *After splitting the points at Didcot, No 08523 derailed and came to rest between two different tracks. Thanks to modern recovery methods of using compressed air jacks, the locomotive was rerailed by a road/rail Bruff unit. These hydraulic jacks can lift a locomotive at one end and by mounting on a traversing table can reposition the locomotive directly back over the track, saving the need to bring expensive and time consuming cranes to the site.*
Darren Ford

Right: *Its useful life over, No 08808, built at BR Derby Works in July 1960, was withdrawn from Carlisle in May 1990. After withdrawal the locomotive was grounded and gutted with components going to keep other locomotives operational. The body shell was eventually sold to Booth-Roe Metals of Rotherham and broken up in March 1992. The remains are seen at Carlisle Upperby.*
Darren Ford

The Diesel Shunter

Left: *In the quest for modernisation, the Class 03s with cut down cabs to work on the BPGV line were replaced by similarly reduced-height Class 08s from 1984. The modification work was carried out at Landore. Prior to renumbering as a Class 08/9, low-height No 08259 is seen on the Coedbach-Cwmmawr line on 16 July 1984 during a test run.*
Tom Clift

Right: *The original three low-height Class 08/9s, Nos 08991-08993 were named after locations on the route in twinning ceremonies held in September 1985 and January 1986. Here two of the trio, Nos 08991* Kidwelly *and 08993* Ashburnham, *stand at Llanelli on 18 January 1986 awaiting official naming by the mayors of the respective towns. The Landore-rebuilt locomotives were given GWR-style cast numbers and nameplates. Modification work included fitting fixed-beam headlights and repositioning the horns to make the locomotives 10 inches lower than a standard Class 08.*
Colin J. Marsden

Left: *To replace 08991/2, a further pair of Class 08/9 conversions, Nos 08994 and 08995 were modified at Landore in 1987. The work followed the same style as the original modifications but included the fitting of air brake only equipment. When not required for freight working over the BPGV line the Class 08/9s were used at Landore depot as pilots, as was the case on 25 January 1993 when No 08994 was photographed 'on shed' with an HST TGS. This locomotive is painted in Railfreight livery.*
Colin J. Marsden

The Diesel Shunter

Above: *Following the take over of the majority of UK rail freight by English Welsh & Scottish Railway, the company livery of maroon and gold was soon applied to locomotives of most classes. The 08/9 fleet was no exception, and No 08993 is seen here shunting at Margam.*
Michael Hill

Below: *After privatisation until the late 1990s, RFS(E) at Doncaster undertook the majority of Class 08 and 09 repairs. Today, however EWS uses the depot at Ferrybridge, just a few miles north of Doncaster, to carry out shunter overhauls. BPGV No 08995 Kidwelly is seen in Transrail livery outside the RFS 'E2' shop at Doncaster in this 19 March 1998 view.*
Colin J. Marsden

Above: *These two rather interesting and perhaps sad cab side views display the end of an era in railway pride. On the left, all that could be done to mark the end of locomotive overhauls at the historic Swindon works was to paint over the position of the original works plate 'Swindons - June 1886 - Final loco' telling the outside works and rail staff that 08616 was the final locomotive to receive classified attention at probably the most famous locomotive works in the world. The other picture on the right shows a cast plate attached to No 08856 marking the final locomotive overhauled at Derby Works.*
R. Jones/Colin J. Marsden

Below: *A number of Class 08s have over the years been named, many after railway staff. Here No 08867 is seen at Darlington with painted on plate* **Ralph Easby***, named after a member of Thornaby depot staff who had completed 50 years railway service.*
Ian S. Carr

The Diesel Shunter

Above: *After privatisation of the railways and the decline in Southern Region shunting work, the Class 09/0 fleet allocated to EWS were used along with the main pool of Class 08 locos, taking the class to new areas of operation. General grey-liveried No 09016 is seen here shunting roller-shutter door-fitted Royal Mail stock at Plymouth on 24 September 2000. This locomotive retains dual brake equipment, complete with high-level air connections.*
Colin J. Marsden

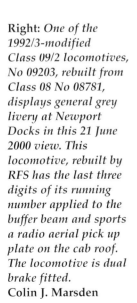

Right: *One of the 1992/3-modified Class 09/2 locomotives, No 09203, rebuilt from Class 08 No 08781, displays general grey livery at Newport Docks in this 21 June 2000 view. This locomotive, rebuilt by RFS has the last three digits of its running number applied to the buffer beam and sports a radio aerial pick up plate on the cab roof. The locomotive is dual brake fitted.*
Colin J. Marsden

The Diesel Shunter

Above: *For the official launch of Trainload Freight at Ripple Lane on 15 October 1987, Stratford-based dual-brake fitted No 08834 was repainted in the then new triple-grey livery and given Railfreight General 'flags' on the rear of the cab side. Complete with Cockney Sparrow cast logo on the bodyside together with a stick-on Sparrow, No 08834 passes Ripple Lane with a demonstration freight for invited guests at the new business launch. This locomotive was a 1960 Derby product and is now owned by Wabtec as a hire loco; during 2003 it was working with GNER.*
Colin J. Marsden

Below: *In the years just prior to privatisation a handful of Class 08s were given extra heavy overhauls at Crewe Works, which involved a total strip and rebuild from the frames upwards. Three Class 08s are seen in the main shop at Crewe on 17 July 1995, with No 08701 nearest the camera.*
Colin J. Marsden

Above: *Aerial view looking down on EWS-liveried No 08957, the penultimate-numbered locomotive of the build, at Newport. This clearly shows the exhaust arrangement at the front. The two roof sections just to the rear of the exhaust port are removable to assist in power unit replacement.*
Colin J. Marsden

Right: *RFS(E) Doncaster was contracted in the 1990s to carry out extensive overhauls to some Class 08s on behalf of EWS and other main line operators. This work involved a total strip down and rebuild, using many new or refurbished components. No 08888 is shown here in the E2 shop at RFS Doncaster on 5 March 1996.*
Colin J. Marsden

Left: *In the period of shadow privatisation with the operation of three Trainload Freight companies — Mainline Freight, Transrail and Loadhaul, several different liveries were applied. Old Oak Common, who looked after some of the Mainline Freight fleet, repainted Class 09 No 09007 into full Mainline Freight 'Aircraft' blue, with bodyside branding in silver. The dual brake-fitted locomotive is seen on the turntable at Old Oak Common. The bottom middle marker light on this locomotive has been plated over rather than removed during its overhaul.*
Darren Ford

Right: *Freightliner, the UK principal container train operator deploys a handful of Class 08s at various terminals. These are mainly hired-in from the private sector. No 08585, painted in full Freightliner livery, is seen at Southampton Maritime terminal. This locomotive is owned by Porterbrook Leasing.*
Andrew Thompson

Left: *Passenger operator Connex, who originally operated the South Central franchise, adopted on privatisation Class 09 No 09025. The locomotive was allocated to Selhurst but in reality was usually found at Brighton depot, where this view of the locomotive in full Connex livery was taken.*
Darren Ford

The Diesel Shunter

Right: EWS-owned dual-brake fitted No 08907 sported LNWR black livery with cast number plates for many years in the 1990s. The locomotive is seen here at Crewe electric depot. No 08907 was built at Horwich Works in July 1962 as No D4137 and spent its entire life working on the London Midland Region.
Darren Ford

Left: Maintrain, the Leeds Neville Hill and Derby-based train maintenance company has a couple of Class 08s for depot pilot operations. No 08690 is shown in full Maintrain livery at Derby Etches Park. This locomotive has acquired a standard high-intensity headlight, as the locomotive frequently goes onto the main line in the Derby area.
Michael Hill

Right: Another of the unusual liveries was applied to Stratford-allocated No 08715 which emerged in 'dayglow' yellow in the mid 1990s. The locomotive was used as pilot at the depot and in this view has gained a Stratford 'Cockney Sparrow' crest on the bodyside and a non-standard spotlight on the front end.
Darren Ford

The Diesel Shunter

Above: *West Coast Traincare, now Alstom, operates a handful of Class 08s from the principal WCML depots at Polmadie, Willesden Longsight and Oxley. These have been painted in a black livery and some carry 'pit-stop' markings. With its 'pit-stop' flag on the side, No 08887 is seen at Willesden DED on 13 February 1998.*
Colin J. Marsden

Centre Left: *In recent years a number of Class 08 and 09 locomotives have been named; these have usually been done by the application of cast plates, fitted to the battery box side panels. Plates are usually manufactured by either Newton Replicas or Procast. The Procast plate* **Pat Barr,** *unveiled on No 08694 at Old Oak Common in August 2000 is illustrated.*
Colin J. Marsden

Left Below: *In the period leading up to privatisation, Rail Express Systems was formed to oversee the operation of the parcels and Royal Mail services. This business unit adopted a red and grey livery scheme, which was applied to main line and shunting power. No 08873 a dual brake locomotive is seen at Crewe Diesel Depot.*
Darren Ford

The Diesel Shunter

Above: *Cardiff-allocated EWS-liveried No 08957 is seen on the dockside at Newport, assisting with the arrival of new EWS Class 66s on 26 August 1998.*
Colin J. Marsden

Centre Right: *Carrying the name* Stephen Dent, *after a Bristol-based railwayman who died in 1997, EWS liveried No 08896 is seen from its radiator end in Didcot yard.*
Darren Ford

Right: *The pioneer member of the Class 09 fleet, No 09001, looking in a rather tatty condition, stands with a PCV Royal Mail formation at Plymouth.*
Darren Ford

The Diesel Shunter

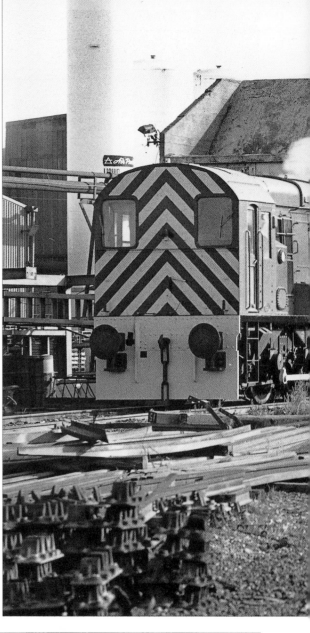

Above: *To enable shunting of Eurostar stock at North Pole depot in West London, Class 08 No 08948 was purchased and rebuilt with drop head Scharfenberg couplers and air-dryers. The modification work which lengthened the locomotive both front and back was undertaken at Crewe Works. The locomotive is seen stabled at North Pole depot.*
Colin J. Marsden

Right: *A large number of withdrawn BR 'standard' 0-6-0 diesel-electric shunting locomotives have found their way into industrial use. Former BR Nos 08133 and 08216 are seen shunting at Sheerness Iron & Steel on 6 September 1984. To improve adhesion, both these locomotives have been given extended buffer beams.*
Les Nixon

Below: *After withdrawal from BR, No 08046 was sold to Associated British Maltsters for use in private sidings at Airdrie. The locomotive is seen repainted in house colours crossing North Calder Viaduct on 16 September 1981.* Colin J. Marsden

Right: *With the splitting up of the rail industry into small business and private units, the major workshops all obtained diesel shunting locomotives for pilot use. The site at Eastleigh, initially run by British Rail Maintenance Ltd, obtained No 08642, the original No D3809. The locomotive was painted in non-authentic LSWR black lined livery and is seen here in the works yard at Eastleigh. After subsequent changes, this locomotive is now owned by Freightliner and at the time of writing is stored at Southampton Maritime terminal. Colin J. Marsden*

The Diesel Shunter

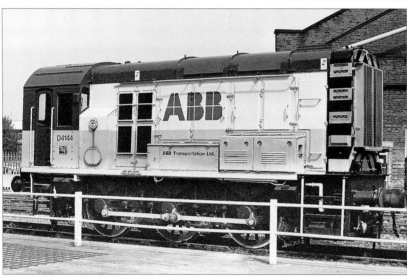

Above: *Wearing ABB-colours, the former Class 08 No 08943 was sold to the engineering company by BR at privatisation for use at major works. The locomotive was passed through the Crewe facility and given a classified overhaul and the ABB identity of 002. Subsequent to ABB, the locomotive has now passed to Bombardier Transportation ownership. The illustration shows the locomotive shunting a 'Networker' Class 465 driving car at York.*
Colin J. Marsden

Centre Left: *A locomotive which has often caused confusion is Class 08 No 08846, the original D4014, which for some reason was renumbered by ABB to D4144, following a classified overhaul and repaint. The locomotive is seen in two-tone grey house colours at Derby Litchurch Lane.*
Colin J. Marsden

Left: *Purchased by Russell for use at their Deanside Transit depot at Hillington, Glasgow, the company obtained four ex-BR Class 08s 08345, 08447, 08728/36. No 08447 is seen fully repainted into high-visibility yellow with Deanside branding and a rather unusual yellow/black wasp end arrangement.*
Colin J. Marsden

The Diesel Shunter

This page: *RFS Industries of Doncaster, the predecessor to Wabtec Doncaster, formed an important locomotive hire business in the 1980s and 1990s, providing a number of private and national operators with traction units, including the engineering firm building the Channel Tunnel. Above is No 002* **Prudence**, *a vacuum brake example which was previously No 08164. The illustration below shows a line of industrial and ex BR shunting locos, led by No RFS 007, the former BR No 08077 inside the RFS 'E2' shop at Doncaster.*
Both: **Colin J. Marsden**

This page: *In 1974 a batch of five redundant ex-Southern Region Class 08s were heavily rebuilt at Derby Works and sold to Lamco Mining of Liberia. The locomotives were modified with air brakes, special headlights on front and back ends and extended draw gear with autocouplers and were then repainted into Lamco orange and white livery and exported via Liverpool Docks to their new home in West Africa. The view left shows the second of the conversions, No D3092, being loaded onto a ship at Liverpool, while the illustration below shows the former No D3098 in the works yard at Derby being tested prior to packing for shipment.*
Both: **Author's collection**

Right and Centre: *The locomotive hire market has become quite lucrative business in the UK since privatisation, with many of the main operators choosing to hire-in shunting power than owning their own expensive assets. Cotswold Rail owns a handful of ex-BR Class 08s, some of which have been given classified overhauls and are now certified for full Railtrack operation. The first of the fleet to carry the distinctive Cotswold grey livery was No 08871, which was overhauled by Brush Traction. The locomotive is seen in the Brush works yard. Another company with huge credibility in the locomotive hire market is Harry Needle Railroad Co (HNRC) who can provide customers with a large range of shunting locos. In the illustration middle right we see No 08818 carrying full HNRC yellow livery on hire to Freightliner at Leeds.*
Colin J. Marsden/Michael Hill

Below: *The preservation movement has also purchased a sizeable number of withdrawn Class 08-10 locomotives and returned them to full main line standards. The West Somerset Railway is home to privately-owned No 08850, a dual brake-fitted locomotive painted in BR rail blue. The locomotive is see on 29 October 1994 shunting at Blue Anchor prior to forming the 13.50 to Minehead.*
Colin J. Marsden

Above: *BR Research at Derby took over Class 08 No 08267 in March 1978 for the development of remote control and automated shunting technology. After much work at Derby the locomotive was transferred to the Mickleover test track where it performed active tests. For its departmental role the Class 08 was renumbered 97801, painted in full BR rail blue livery and given the name* Pluto.
Colin J. Marsden

Below: *Polmadie depot in Glasgow, Scotland converted Class 08 No 08173 to an internal depot pilot locomotive from May 1978 and renumbered the BR blue locomotive PO1 (Polmadie 1). The locomotive remained in use as a depot pilot until withdrawn in September 1984. It was eventually sold to V. Berry and broken up at BR Thornton Junction. On 13 August 1983 the locomotive is seen at Polmadie.*
John Hillmer

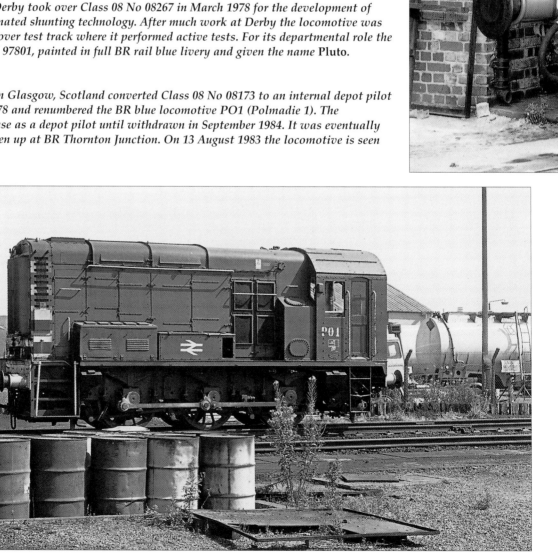

Above: *Slade Green depot on the Southern Region, which housed a major regional workshop and collision repair facility, took over Class 08 No 08600 in May 1979 as a workshop pilot. The depot repainted the locomotive in departmental red/blue livery and named it* Ivor *in June 1979. After many years in departmental use at Slade Green, the locomotive returned to the capital stock fleet, resuming its former identity of 08600 from March 1990.* Ivor *is seen on shed at Slade Green.*
Colin J. Marsden

Right: *To power the Severn Tunnel emergency train kept at Sudbrook, BR had to always keep an operational locomotive on hand. After a period of using a PWM shunter, Class 09 No 09017 was taken over in October 1987 as a dedicated emergency train locomotive. It was soon renumbered into the departmental series as No 97806. The locomotive, in BR blue with a grey cab and red sole bar, is seen at Newport. The locomotive was returned to its Class 09 identity in July 1997.*
Darren Ford

The Diesel Shunter

BR Workshops 0-6-0+0-6-0 diesel-electric
D4500-D4502
Class 13
13001-13003

Three of the most bizarre locomotives classified as 'shunting' power, were the 0-6-0+0-6-0 twin units, each formed of a modified pair of Class 08s.

The three locomotives were modified and formed by BR Darlington Works in May-July 1965 for hump shunting operations at Tinsley yard in Sheffield.

The rebuilding work saw one locomotive of each semi-permanently coupled pair have its cab removed, while extra weight 'plates' were welded to the buffer beams of both locos. Initially one slave and one master locomotive were coupled cab to cab with the remaining driving cab in the centre. Later due to sighting problems on the Tinsley hump, the pairings were reformed with the slave coupled ahead of the master locomotive in elephant style.

Control over both locomotives was placed under the driver on the master loco, with full multiple unit control equipment fitted in terms of both electric and pneumatic connections. The starting of the slave locomotive was done from the master locomotive's cab.

When first modified all three locomotives were numbered in the D4500-02 series and painted in BR locomotive green livery, wasp ends were applied at the outer ends. Classified overhaul post-1978 saw all three emerge from Doncaster Works painted in standard rail blue livery. After 1973 all three were renumbered into the five digit TOPS range as Class 13, Nos 13003/1/2 respectively.

The demise of much of the traffic in the early 1980s saw one locomotive, No 13002, withdrawn from capital stock in 1981. The other pair soldiered on until 1985 when hump shunting at Tinsley ceased. Sadly none of the three locomotives was saved for preservation.

Vacuum train brakes were fitted, no provision being made for air braking, and electric marker lights were provided as in Class 08 days.

The driving cabs of these locomotives were modified during the conversion work from Class 08 to 13 to incorporate a radio telephone system allowing the hump drivers to have contact with the control tower.

Below: Coupled in the original configuration — cab to cab end — No D4502 stands outside Tinsley depot in Sheffield on 15 July 1965, prior to entering service. This 'loco' is formed of former Class 08s Nos D4187 and D3697. The livery applied is BR standard green, with full wasp ends.
Author's collection

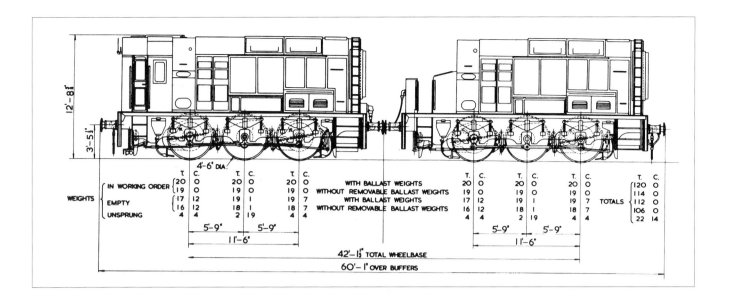

TOPS number range: 13001-13003
1957 BR number range: D4500-D4502
Former class code: 7/1
Rebuilt by: BR Darlington (Note: 1)
Year introduced: 1965
Wheel arrangement: 0-6-0 + 0-6-0
Weight: 120 tons
Height: 12ft 8⅝in
Length: 60ft 1in
Width: 8ft 6in
Wheelbase: 8ft 7¼in
Wheel diameter: 3ft 6in
Min curve negotiable: Originally: 3 chains, Modified: 2½ chains

Engine type: 2 x EE 6K
Engine output: Total: 700hp
Power at rail: Total: 320hp
Tractive effort: 70,000lb
Cylinder bore: 10in
Cylinder stroke: 12in
Maximum speed: 20mph
Brake type: Air on loco, Vacuum on train
Brake force: 64¾ tons
Route availability: 8
Heating type: Not fitted
Multiple coupling type: Within type only
Main generator type: EE801-8E
Aux generator type: EE736-2D

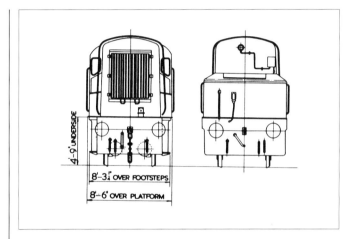

Traction motor type: EE506-6A
No of traction motors: 4
Gear ratio: 23.9:1
Fuel tank capacity: Total: 1,336gal
Cooling water capacity: Total: 280gal
Lub oil capacity: Total: 90gal
Sanding equipment: Pneumatic

Note
1: Formed of two Class 08s, semi-permanently coupled. When first introduced coupled cab to cab, formation then revised to operate cab to nose.

Right: *Working towards the hump in Tinsley low level yard, No D4500 is seen in August 1965, soon after taking up operation. It is interesting to note that the cab end of the master was not painted in wasp colours, and that no BR logo was applied to the slave loco.*
Colin J. Marsden

Above: *Marshalled in the revised 'elephant style', No D4501 is seen at Doncaster Works after reformation. This picture shows the extra thickness of the buffer beam to increase adhesive weight. After reforming to be coupled nose to cab, the cab ends of the master units were given wasp markings and the British Railways logo was applied to the battery box of the slave unit.* **Derek Porter**

Left: *The driving cab of the 'master' locomotive was modified to house a special design speedometer unit and ammeter display, which provided the driver with the performance of the 'slave' unit. Additionally, the locomotives were fitted with a unique slow speed control function for propelling trains over the Tinsley hump, and a separate speedometer calibrated down to 20ths of a mile per hour was fitted. To provide communication between the locomotive and hump signal box a cab-shore radio system was also fitted below the speedometer, while a light box signal system was fitted above, which if showing a horizontal line of three lights meant stop, a vertical display meaning proceed and a group at 45 deg — slow down.* **Colin J. Marsden**

The Diesel Shunter

Above: *Although converted at Darlington Works, the 'Master & Slave' or Class 13 shunters were looked after at Doncaster Works. In this 10 September 1977 view, No 13002 is seen undergoing a classified overhaul, which included a repaint from BR green to BR blue livery.*
Colin J. Marsden

Above: *Viewed from its 'Slave' end, No 13002 is seen in the depot yard at Tinsley on 8 August 1979. By this time the livery applied was 'standard'.*
Colin J. Marsden

Right: *Looking rather tatty or perhaps sun scorched, No 13001 stands with a brakevan in the low level yard at Tinsley on 15 April 1983. This locomotive, although painted in BR blue, did not have wasp ends applied to the nose end of the 'Master' unit.*
J. H. G. Saunders

The Diesel Shunter

Left: *With the Tinsley steam crane parked in the background, 'Master & Slave' Nos 13001 and 13003 stand in the main diesel depot yard in this 6 October 1984 view. By this time the locomotives' work was in terminal decline. Both locomotives were withdrawn in January 1985.*
John Rudd

Below: *The hump yards at Tinsley only operated on weekdays and some Saturday mornings, so most weekends the 'Master & Slave' sets could be found stabled on shed at Tinsley. No 13001 is seen on the high level yard fuel bay in this 28 February 1982 view.*
Colin J. Marsden

Right: *Awaiting the instruction to move forward to collect the next train for 'humping' Class 13 No 13003 sits on the brow of the hump in this October 1979 view.*
Colin J. Marsden

Below: *Normally the Class 13s would never be involved in passenger operations, so on 7 October 1978 a Sheffield Merrymaker charter was operated and used a class member for one leg of its Mexborough-Chesterfield-Tinsley-Dinting-York-Sheffield route. No 13003 is seen passing under the 1,500V dc electric network at Rotherwood Sidings, Orgreave, near Sheffield.*
Les Nixon

BR Swindon 0-6-0 diesel-hydraulic - Type 1
D9500-D9555
Class 14

These centre-cab 650hp diesel-hydraulic locomotives, given the Type 1 classification were primarily designed for shunting operations, with the ability to undertake short main line duties or trip workings.

Sadly the locomotives were ordered far too late in the day to be of any major success. Between the time the 56 strong fleet was ordered by BR and construction at Swindon, most of the work identified for the fleet had been lost. The fleet was thus born into a very uncertain railway world.

The locomotives were of conventional construction, with a main underframe assembly and two deep weight-based buffer beams at each end. The drive from the hydraulic transmission to the linked wheels was by the jackshaft arrangement.

The slightly off-centre cab of this design was full width, with a central driving position, giving the driver good all-round visibility of operations. The longer of the two bonnet sections housed the Paxman 6YJXL engine, which drove an under cab transmission supplied by Voith.

The two nose sections were fitted with hinged inspection doors giving access to all equipment. The roof of the sections was also removable to allow easy access to larger items.

To allow for main line trip workings, these locomotives were fitted with four-character route indicator panels and had a top speed of 40mph.

Upon construction the locomotives were painted in a very neat two-tone green colour, the cab being a light green and the nose sections a dark shade. Running numbers were applied in transfer form on the cab sides in the D95xx series and a carriage-style Lion over Crown roundel was applied above the number.

Braking was provided by vacuum for trains and straight air on the locomotive. Multiple control equipment was not provided.

The first locomotive of the fleet emerged from Swindon in July 1964 with all 56 delivered by October 1965. By late 1967, just two years after delivery, the first examples were withdrawn and by 1969 the entire fleet had gone, purely as surplus to requirements. In 1965 the BRB were seeking purchasers for the fleet and several attempts were made to sell the entire fleet to an overseas buyer. However as time came to prove, the vast majority entered industrial service. In later years a number have found their way into the hands of preservationists, with several locomotives in fully operational condition.

Below: Parked in the middle road at Reading on 7 August 1965, No D9522 is viewed from its short bonnet end while resting between station pilot duties. This locomotive was delivered in November 1964 to Old Oak Common shed and withdrawn just 37 months later and broken up.
A. Swain

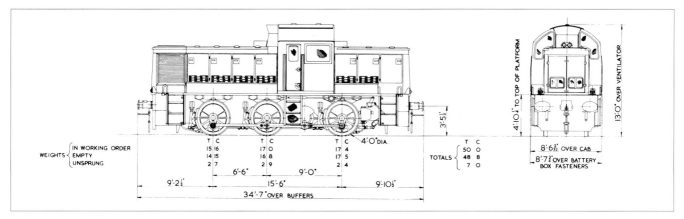

Former class code:	6/1	Tractive effort:	30,910lb
Built by:	BR Swindon	Cylinder bore:	7in
Year introduced:	1964-65	Cylinder stroke:	7³/₄in
Wheel arrangement:	0-6-0	Maximum speed:	40mph
Weight:	50 tons	Brake type:	Air on loco,vacuum on train
Height:	10ft 0in	Brake force:	32 tonnes
Length:	34ft 7in	Route availability:	2
Width:	8ft 7¹/₂in	Heating type:	Not fitted
Wheelbase:	15ft 6in	Multiple coupling type:	Not fitted
Wheel diameter:	4ft 0in	Transmission	Hydraulic — Voith L217u
Min curve negotiable:	3 chains	Fuel tank capacity:	338gal
Engine type:	Paxman 6YJXL 'Ventura'	Cooling water capacity:	104gal
Engine output:	650hp	Lub oil capacity:	25gal
Power at rail:	405hp	Sanding equipment:	Pneumatic

Below: Assembly of this short-lived fleet was undertaken in the great Swindon 'A' shop, with around 20 locomotives at a time under assembly. This view shows the pioneer locomotive of the fleet under assembly, with four others in various stages of production. No D9500 is seen from the non-engine end. In the foreground is one of the Paxman 6YJXL 'Ventura' power units. In the background behind the new build line is a Class 47 receiving attention.
Author's collection

Above: *In the days when 'trip' freights still operated, No D9522 departs from Reading on 30 January 1965 with a coal train for Earley yard.*
A. Swain

Below: *A quite wonderful view of the production line at Swindon, showing no fewer than five 0-6-0 Type 1s under assembly, with main line diesel-hydraulics under repair in the rear. This picture is dated 21 September 1964.*
Author's collection

The Diesel Shunter

This page: *Thankfully the preservation movement has taken over a number of the BR Class 14 or 'Teddy Bear' locomotives as they have become known. Most of these have been obtained through industrial users, who took sizeable quantities of locomotives when withdrawn in the mid-1960s. In the view above, locomotives D9526 and D9551 pose for the camera at Minehead. In spring 2003, No D9526 was returned to traffic after a major rebuild and should be a regular performer on the railway for many years to come. In the view below, No D9521 is seen at the Swanage Railway, painted in National Coal Board livery and awaiting restoration.*
Both: Colin J. Marsden

Trials Locomotives

D0226, D0227

Original number:	D226	D227
Revised number:	D0226	D0227
Built by:	English Electric	English Electric
Year introduced:	1956	1956
Wheel arrangement:	0-6-0	0-6-0
Weight:	47 tons	48 tons
Height:	12ft 3in	12ft 3in
Length:	31ft 8½in	31ft 8½in
Width:	8ft 10in	8ft 10in
Wheelbase:	13ft 0in	13ft 0in
Wheel diameter:	4ft 0in	4ft 0in
Min curve negotiable:	4½ chains	4½ chains
Engine type:	English Electric 6RKT	English Electric 6RKT
Engine output:	500hp	500hp
Power at rail:	360hp	360hp
Tractive effort:	33,000lb	33,000lb
Cylinder bore:	10in	10in
Cylinder stroke:	12in	12in
Maximum speed:	40mph	40mph
Brake type:	Vacuum	Vacuum
Brake force:	30 tons	30 tons
Route availability:	Not issued	Not issued
Heating type:	Not fitted	Not fitted
Multiple coupling type:	Not fitted	Not fitted
Transmission type:	Diesel electric	Diesel hydraulic
Main generator type:	EE824-1B	-
Aux generator type :	EE	-
Traction motor type:	EE607A	-
Transmission type:	-	Krupp 3 WD 46
No of traction motors:	2	-
Gear ratio:	8.13:1	-
Fuel tank capacity:	545gal	545gal
Lub oil capacity:	55gal	55gal
Sanding equipment:	Pneumatic	Pneumatic

The English Electric Co built two 500hp diesel trip/shunting locomotives for BTC trials in 1956, in an attempt to provide a second generation of shunting power — which was of course not required. The two locomotives were numbered D226 and D227, and although looking very similar, were technically quite different. No D226 was a diesel-electric, while No D227 was a diesel-hydraulic. Construction of the locomotives was carried out at Vulcan Foundry, Newton-le-Willows and after completion and static trials, were sent to Stratford in East London for BTC approval and testing. Soon after delivery to Stratford, the applied numbering clashed with EE Type 4s, allocated to the depot and an '0' was added in front of the running number providing the identities of D0226 and D0227. In the English Electric order book, the locomotives were shown as heavy haul pilots and road locomotives with a top speed of 40mph.

Below: *Its side doors removed, No D226 is seen in the yard at Vulcan Foundry soon after construction, clearly showing the English Electric RKT power unit. This was centrally mounted over the leading two axles, while the generator unit was mounted towards the cab, gaining ventilation from grilles in the bodyside doors. At the front of the locomotive was a radiator and fan group. The fuel tank was to the rear of the cab, perhaps not a good place if a collision had occurred!*
Author's collection

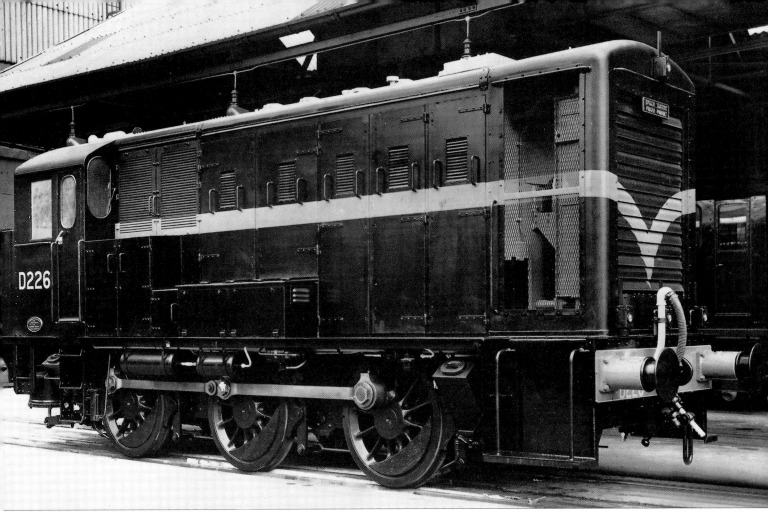

This page: *These two further views of No D226 show both sides of the locomotive from the nose end, following the full application of livery. This was based on all-over black, offset by an orange mid-height band, finishing on the front radiator in a downward chevron. This was another early attempt at a front end warning, making the otherwise black end distinctive from a distance. Vacuum train braking was provided as standard and electric front and rear marker lights were provided. The boxes on the sole plate contained the vacuum exhauster and starting batteries.*
Both: **Author's collection**

The Diesel Shunter

This page: *The second locomotive of the English Electric trial pair, No D227 (D0227) was the diesel-hydraulic machine. The same English Electric RKT engine was fitted but this drove a Krupp 3 WD 46 transmission. Performance of the hydraulic locomotive was never on par with the diesel-electric, but records from Stratford show the locomotives' availability to have been around 70%. The livery on D227 was the same as that applied to D226. Both locomotives were withdrawn in 1959. No D0226 was later sold to the Keighley & Worth Valley Railway where it is still in use today. No D0227 was sadly broken up in July 1964 at the RSH works in Darlington. Both:* **Author's collection**

The Diesel Shunter

Janus and Taurus

Name:	Taurus	Janus
Number:	-	-
Built by:	Yorkshire Engine Co	Yorkshire Engine Co
Years introduced:	1961	1956
Wheel arrangement:	0-8-0	0-6-0
Weight:	56 tons	48 tons
Height:	12ft 2in	12ft 2in
Length:	31ft 11$^{1}/_{4}$in	24ft 11in
Width:	8ft 5$^{1}/_{2}$in	8ft 5$^{1}/_{2}$in
Wheelbase:	13ft 6in	9ft 3in
Wheel diameter:	3ft 9in	3ft 9n
Min curve negotiable:	4 chains	3 chains
Engine type:	2 x Rolls Royce 8SFL	2 x Rolls Royce 8SFL
Engine output:	600hp	400hp
Power at rail:	450hp	290hp
Tractive effort:	45,000lb	30,000lb
Cylinder bore:	5$^{1}/_{2}$in	5$^{1}/_{2}$in
Cylinder stroke:	6in	6in
Maximum speed:	36mph	23mph
Brake type:	Air on loco, vacuum train brakes	Air on loco, -
Brake force:	35 tonnes	35 tonnes
Route availability:	Not issued	Not issued
Heating type:	Not fitted	Not fitted
Multiple coupling type:	Not fitted	Not fitted
Transmission type:	Hydraulic	Hydraulic
Fuel tank capacity:	450gal	400gal
Gear ratio:	9.875:1	§
Lub oil capacity:	45gal	40gal
Sanding equipment:	Pneumatic	Pneumatic

The Yorkshire Engine Co was another of the main industrial locomotive builders of the 1950s which was very keen to enter the mass markets of producing main line shunting and trip locomotives. Various attempts were made to offer heavy 0-6-0 and 0-8-0 units to the BTC, but apart from trials nothing came to fruition. Two locomotives were however given authorisation for limited trials in selected BTC yards. One, an 0-8-0, was identified at *Taurus* and the other, an 0-6-0, as *Janus*. In both cases this name was the Yorkshire Engine Co's product name rather than the identity of a specific locomotive.

Below: *Side elevation of the* **Janus** *product line, showing an 0-6-0 48 ton single cab unit. Traction was provided by a pair of Rolls Royce 8SFL engines one mounted in each bonnet section. In traditional industrial style access to the driving cab was via end steps and a walkway along the side of the engine compartment.*
Author's collection

Above: The **Janus** *production type also extended to a diesel-electric version, which was built for the Appleby-Frodingham steel Company of Scunthorpe. While the locomotive is a true industrial, it serves as a good illustration of the body style of the design, with deep thick buffer beams to add adhesive weight, and a barrow walkway to the cab from the steps at the locomotive end. Driving controls were arranged on both sides of the cab, allowing a good all round view of operations. This view of the Scunthorpe locomotive is seen at the builder's factory in Shrewsbury.*
Author's collection

Below: *One of the* **Janus** *diesel-hydraulic products was used for a short period in the Sheffield area, where it is seen here with a rake of wooden bodied wagons. This locomotive is painted in a dark (almost BR) green.*
Author's collection

The Diesel Shunter

This page: *Two views of the larger 0-8-0* Taurus, *built by Yorkshire Engine Co and offered to the BTC/BR as a main line trip locomotive. The design had two Rolls Royce prime movers, one in each bonnet section, driving a central hydraulic transmission.* Taurus *was certified by the BTC and performed limited trials at Doncaster Works, Stratford and in the Bristol Docks area. The upper view shows the locomotive at its builder's works, while the plate below is the official Yorkshire Engine Co works picture. Note that standard BR vacuum brake equipment was fitted.*
Both: Author's collection

The Diesel Shunter

Departmental Locomotives

PWM650-PWM654

Original number range:	PWM650-PWM654	Engine type:	Ruston 6VPHL
TOPS number range:	97650-97654	Engine horsepower:	165hp at 1,250rpm
CCE plant number:	83650-83654	Main generator type:	BTH RTB6034
Wheel arrangement:	0-6-0	Traction motor type:	BTH RTA5041H
Builder:	Ruston & Hornsby	Tractive effort:	17,000lb
Year introduced:	PWM650 - 1953	Maximum speed:	20mph
	PWM651-PWM654 - 1959	Brake type (loco):	Air
Length:	24ft 8½in	Brake type (train):	PWM650 - None/Vacuum later fitted
Height:	11ft 0in		PWM651-654 - Vacuum
Width:	8ft 6in	Ruston order number:	PWM650 - 51/510343
Route availability:	1		PWM651-PWM654 -
Weight:	PWM650 - 28 tons		51/580102-51/580105
	PWM651-654 - 30 tons	Ruston Works numbers:	PWM650 - 312990
Wheel diameter:	PWM650 - 3ft 2½in		PWM651-PWM654 - 431758-431761
	PWM651-654 - 3ft 4in		

Below: The pioneer locomotive of the Western Region Permanent Way Machinery (PWM) fleet of 0-6-0 Ruston shunters, No PWM650. This loco, built some six years prior to the rest of the fleet was slightly different in body design to the rest of the class. Many of these are quite apparent if this and the illustration opposite (bottom) are compared. Areas of change included the radiator grille, front end footsteps, cab window design, warning horn position, windscreen wipers and the front buffer beam. **CJM collection**

The Diesel Shunter

This page: *In the six years between the delivery of the first locomotive and of the other four, a number of changes were deemed necessary. Perhaps the most noticeable from these two views is that the livery is BR locomotive green rather than BR black applied to PWM650. Also vacuum brakes are seen to have been fitted. The illustration above shows No PWM653 at Swindon Works on 27 September 1959, awaiting official commissioning. Slight variations appear to have taken place even during the construction of the four 'production' locos, with No PWM653 showing an exhaust stack, whereas No PWM651 illustrated below in the Ruston Works yard at Lincoln, does not show this fitting. In terms of Ruston & Hornsby, this design of small 0-6-0 locomotive was also available with a 0-4-0 wheel arrangement and was straight out of the company's industrial catalogue. J. A. Coiley/CJM collection*

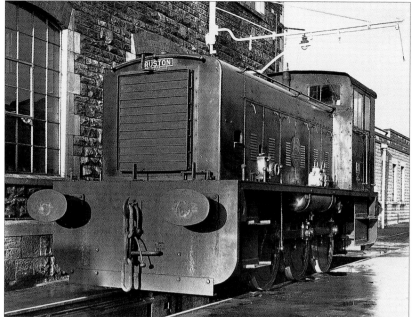

Left: *It is interesting that by the time this illustration of the pioneer No PWM650 had been taken on 6 November 1955 at Swindon Works, some quite major structural changes had been made. The nose end radiator is now covered with a hinged flap panel, and a mechanical lubricator has been mounted on the front of the running plate, connecting down to the leading wheelset. The Lion over Wheel logo in the middle of the body now appears to be applied to a separate panel, rather than applied direct to the body side as in the opening illustration of this section.* Brian Morrison

Right: *Still painted in BR black livery, No PWM650 is seen at Wellington (Salop) on 2 January 1958, while engaged in engineering works. The additional mechanical lubricator is clearly visible in this illustration.* Author's collection

Below: *Yellow/black wasp warning ends were progressively applied in the late 1960s and early 1970s, and were wrapped around the side of the radiator end in the same style as a Class 03 or 08. No PWM651 is seen at Radyr in South Wales, usually a home for one of the PWMs, on 8 December 1973.* Norman Preedy

The Diesel Shunter

Above: *It is always surprising that the flimsy little 'headlight' mounted on the top centre of the radiator was not frequently knocked off, but the pictures we have seem to show the light firmly intact. With an additional oil headlight on the centre lamp iron, No PWM651 is seen at Reading in November 1958. T. C. Lawrence*

Left: *Soon after delivery in 1959, No PWM652 is seen 'on shed' at Westbury depot. At the rear of the locomotive is a withdrawn steam locomotive tender being used for scrap reclamation. R. S. Carpenter*

Right: *This rear end view of pioneer No PWM650 shows the very much smaller rear cab windows. By the time this picture was taken inside Reading depot in 1989, the locomotive looked in poor condition, but was at least painted in standard BR rail blue and carried its TOPS number 97650 on the bodyside. Reading was always a location where the PWMs could be found either working or receiving maintenance. Colin J. Marsden*

The Diesel Shunter

Left Top: *By the early 1990s, the PWM fleet had lost their PWM prefixed numbers and were known by their TOPS Class 97 identities. No 97654, the former PWM654, is seen painted in all-over engineers' yellow, a colour applied to all locomotives after 1991, as by then the fleet were deemed as 'on track plant' rather than locomotives. By this time it also became rare to find the locomotives operating on the main line, with trips between worksites usually being in the consist of an engineers train.* **Darren Ford**

Centre Left: *Another view of the same locomotive as in the previous illustration, 97654, but taken from the front end to show how the yellow livery was applied to the nose section. The small headlight was retained, but two battery powered marker lights were now fitted above the buffers.* **Darren Ford**

Below: *The disposal of the PWMs commenced in 1990, when No 97652 was cut up at Laira, Plymouth. All others still remain. No 97650 is preserved on the Grimsby & Louth Railway, 97651 on the Northampton & Lamport Line, 97653 by The Yorkshire Engine Co, while No 97654 is operated by Jarvis Rail. No 97653 is seen here just before removal from Reading for preservation, by the looks of this picture, preservation might have been a long and costly project.* **Darren Ford**

The Diesel Shunter

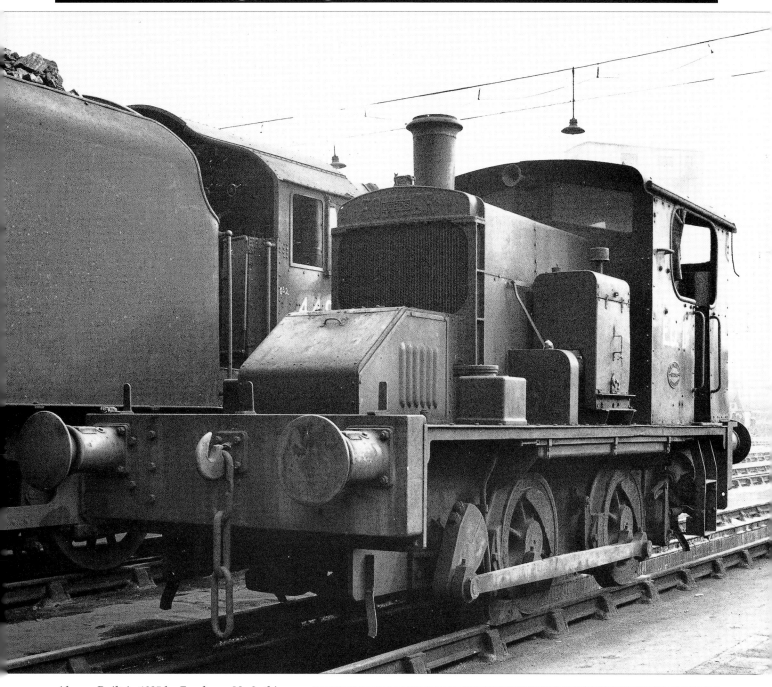

Above: *Built in 1935 by Fowler as No 2, this little 0-4-0 became Engineering Department 1 (ED1) in April 1949 being based at Castleton engineering depot; it moved to Beeston in 1960 and to Derby Works in 1962, and was withdrawn and dismantled in mid-1962. On 23 August 1955, the locomotive is seen on shed at Patricroft.* **Brian Morrison**

Right: *The standard design of 'ED' series small 0-4-0 shunter, of which six were built, were numbered ED2 to ED6 (built 1949) and ED7 (1940). No ED2, seen here at Derby on 30 November 1958, was usually used at the Ditton engineers site, its return to Derby being for workshop attention. The rods have been removed to facilitate rail transit.* **Author's collection**

Left: *Another view of No ED2 at Derby shows the front of the engine end. The livery is standard BR black, with a Lion over Wheel logo on the engine room side. No train brakes were provided. The total output from the Fowler engine was 150bhp, running at 1,000rpm. No ED2 was eventually withdrawn at Derby in 1965 and broken up two years later.*
Author's collection

Right: *With a hand pump attached to the front of the body, a very decrepit-looking ED3 is inside Toton depot on 16 March 1958. At the time this locomotive was working from Castleton civil engineers depot. The locomotive remained in service until 1967, working for its final three years at Bedford.*
P. J. Sharpe

Left: *With its Fowler engine visible through the open engine room side doors, No ED4, introduced in 1949 for use at Northampton Engineers' Depot. From June 1963 the locomotive moved to Derby Works where it remained until withdrawn the following year. While still in full operational condition, No ED4 visited Derby Works in February 1960 for a classified overhaul, and is seen here on 28 February in company with an English Electric Type 1.*
R. H. Wells

The Diesel Shunter

Right: *With the rather unusual sliding cab door in the open position, No ED4 is seen at Northampton in early 1960. Like many of the early small shunting locomotives extra weight for adhesion was provided by thick buffer beams.* Author's collection

Below: *No ED5 was used at Beeston between 1949-55 and at Castleton between 1955-60. It is seen still with British Railways brandings in 1961.* Author's collection

The Diesel Shunter

Left: *Displaying black livery with a red buffer beam and with British Railways branding, No ED5 is seen in almost ex-works condition in June 1959 outside Derby Works, the only major workshop which undertook repairs on the ED fleet.*
R. J. Buckley

Left: *Viewed from its short or non-engine end, No ED6, painted in BR green livery is seen inside Newton Heath depot, Manchester in 1961. At this time the locomotive was experiencing major trouble with its engine, which had been removed and returned to J. Fowler for attention.*
A. Whitworth

Below: *Having receiving a classified overhaul at Derby in May 1960, ED6 went to Castleton engineers yard, where it is seen in green livery with Lion over Crown logo on 25 May 1961 prior to going to Newton Heath*
I. Holt

Above: *Sharing depot space with a DMMU, No ED6 is seen on shed at Newton Heath in 1959. The livery is black with a full British Railways legend on the engine bonnet side.*
J. Wilkinson

Below: *In ex-works BR green with Lion over Crown logo facing forward, No ED6 with some rather non-standard numbers is seen on shed at Newton Heath following overhaul at Derby in mid-1960.*
J. Wilkinson

The Diesel Shunter

Left: *In a rather unusual lined green livery, with a British Railways logo too big for the space between the lining on the cab side, Departmental No 84 is seen at its home depot of York in 1967. The locomotive was built by Ruston to an industrial design in 1959.*
D. Talbot

The Diesel Shunter

Left: *Eastern Region Departmental Locomotive No 81 is a rather interesting little locomotive. It was purpose-built for the Eastern Region engineers department by Andrew Barclay in 1958 and delivered to Peterborough depot, and then transferred to Cambridge a couple of years later. By the mid-1960s it became redundant from engineering use and it was agreed that as the locomotive was basically a BR Class 01, it would be taken into capital stock as a member of this fleet. Very unusually it was given the running number, D2956, of a previously-withdrawn class member on 2 July 1967, making this one of the few numbers on a 'modern traction' locomotive to have been used twice. In immaculate ex-works BR green livery, No 81 is seen posing for its official Andrew Barclay photograph.*
Author's collection

Right: *Another of the purpose-built Eastern Region Departmental locomotives is No 83, built by Ruston in 1959, which operated in Low Fell civil engineers' yard from Gateshead depot. The locomotive was stored in October 1969 and withdrawn in May 1970, being broken up at Attercliffe later the same year.*
Ian Carr

The Diesel Shunter

Above: *Looking rather forlorn inside York shed in the company of an 'A4' Pacific, BR North Eastern Region Civil Engineering Department No 84 takes a rest from yard shunting at Leeman Road on 15 March 1964. With its side doors removed it looks as if engine repairs were being undertaken.*
K. Till

Below: *Two of the 'large' Hunslet 0-6-0 diesel-mechanical shunters, Nos D2612 and D2615 (later Class 05), were taken into departmental stock in 1961 and 1964 and numbered 88 and 89. No 88 was allocated to Ayr for use at Barassie and is seen here in the depot yard in very shabby green livery on 4 September 1966.*
P. Foster

Right: *A little diesel locomotive which often generated much interest was No 20, built by Ruston for use at Reading signal works, this was probably the smallest locomotive to be allowed to traverse the main line, frequently seen passing through Reading station when travelling between signal works and depot. No 20 entered service in 1957 painted in black livery with a Lion on Wheel logo on the cab side. The locomotive is seen here parked up between shunts in the signal and telegraph yard.* Darren Ford collection

Left: *Travelling over the main through line at Reading station, No 20 painted in corporate rail blue with wasp ends and a double arrow logo is seen on 5 July 1978. No 20 remained working in the same yard until withdrawn in April 1981 when replaced by a departmental Class 06. However it continued working until mid-1982 after which No 20 was broken up.* Richard Charlson

Right: *No 20 was renumbered into the BR departmental series as No 97020 in May 1980. The locomotive was not through brake fitted and was basically an off-the-shelf Ruston industrial locomotive. It is seen here from its radiator end in the signal works during August 1975.* Ian Allan Library

The Diesel Shunter

SR — Departmental series

Left: *Built by Fowler in 1941 for departmental use on the Southern Region, 400S, later renumbered to DS400, was used largely at Southampton Docks, where this illustration was taken on 31 July 1954. The locomotive was built to works number 22934, and was an 0-4-0 diesel-mechanical unit.*
A. R. Carpenter

Right & Below: *A second Fowler 0-4-0 diesel-mechanical locomotive was No 600s, later DS600, which was built in 1943 for use by the Royal Ordnance Factory at Thorpe Marsh and was later transferred to the Southern Railway in December 1947. In April 1948 the locomotive became No 600s and from mid-1949 was renumbered to DS600. It remained operating at Eastleigh Works until the end of 1964. The view right shows the locomotive at Eastleigh Carriage Works on 3 August 1955, while the picture below taken at the Carriage Works in August 1964 shows the locomotive in BR(SR) green.*
T. Gough/John Bird

This page: *One of the more unusual little shunters was DS1169, built in 1946 by Ruston & Hornsby of Lincoln. It was supplied to the Bristol Aviation Company and taken into BTC stock on the Southern Region on 11 December 1948. It was originally used for civil engineering shunting at Folkestone and then moved to Broad Clyst sleeper depot in Devon in the autumn of 1959. The locomotive passed to the Western Region in 1962 and spent a period at Yeovil until withdrawal in 1971. The picture above shows the loco at Yeovil Junction in March 1968, while the view below was taken at Broad Clyst in July 1962.*
John Cornelius/P. Bertram

The Diesel Shunter

This page: *The locomotive which became DS1173, was built as a demonstrator by Drewry Car Co in 1947 and used at a number of locations during the development and testing of diesel-mechanical shunting traction. In October 1948 the locomotive was sent to the Southern Region and used for testing at the civil engineers yard at Hither Green. The locomotive was eventually sold to the BTC on 20 November 1948 and numbered DS1173. It operated from a number of depots including Hither Green, Brighton and Eastleigh. In March 1967, the locomotive was taken out of Departmental service and allocated fleet number D2341, as numerically the last of the Class 04 Drewry build. The locomotive remained on the Southern Region until finally withdrawn in 1969 and sold for scrap. In the upper view, DS1173 is seen at Brighton, sharing depot space with steam locomotives 32139 and 32575. At this time DS1173 was painted in black livery. The middle illustration shows it in BR green livery at Eastleigh on 3 September 1960, while the picture below shows the locomotive at the end of a shunting move at Hither Green on 18 May 1957. G. Wheeler, R. Dent, John Faulkner*

The Diesel Shunter

Right: *One of the most unusual British Railways-owned shunting locomotives was this narrow gauge works shunter, ZM32, built by Ruston & Hornsby which entered BR service at Horwich in October 1957. The 18in gauge locomotive is seen at Horwich in this August 1959 illustration, behind ZM32 is the similarly-gauged steam works pilot* Wren.
T. K. Widd

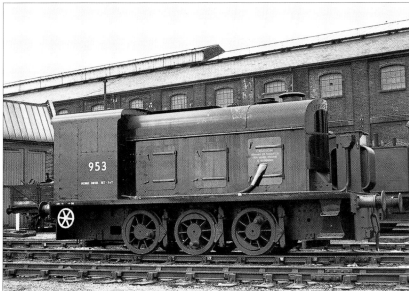

Left: *After withdrawal LMS prototype shunter No 7055 entered BR departmental service as a mobile power plant. The driving cab was sealed up and the locomotive became a hauled vehicle. It was renumbered MPU2, and later 953, after conversion and is seen here in the depot yard at Stratford in June 1955.*
Brian Morrison

What might have been?

Right: *In 1987 consideration was given by BR to replacing the ageing Class 08-09 locomotive fleet, developing a dual role locomotive which could act as a local light freight locomotive for the main line, as well as performing yard shunting duties. The Thomas Hill Group of Rotherham developed detailed plans for a single off-centre cab 1000hp diesel-electric or diesel-hydraulic locomotive, based on a two-axle fixed frame. This drawing was produced by the company to accompany the detailed proposal, however nothing of the project materialised.*

Shunter driving cabs

Above: *Although the rail industry was keen to upgrade their operations using diesel traction, the driving cab on these 'new' locomotives was far from comfortable for the poor driver, with a cluttered working environment, with many protruding items which did not offer the driver a lot of safety in the event of a 'rough shunt'. The view above shows one of the 0-6-0 standard design LMS-built locomotives. The driving desk is set out for operation from both the left and right side, the master position being on the right.* **Author's collection**

Above: *Cab view of standard BR 0-6-0 diesel-electric shunter, showing the master side controller, incorporating the start switch, which also served as the forward and reverse selector. The main amp meter and speedometer in the centre attached to the bulkhead was hinged to enable the driver to angle the display to coincide with his driving position. The chains hanging across the cab operated the warning whistle or horn, while the bulkhead-mounted handle valve operated the pneumatic sanding equipment.* Author's collection

Right: *To facilitate safe and easy working in some of the bigger marshalling yards an early form of cab-to-shore radio was fitted into some BR standard 0-6-0s. This view shows a driver holding the telephone handset, which was connected to a control box below the amp and speedometer. It is worth noting that in this cab an inspection light is plugged into the cab's power socket.* Author's collection

The Diesel Shunter

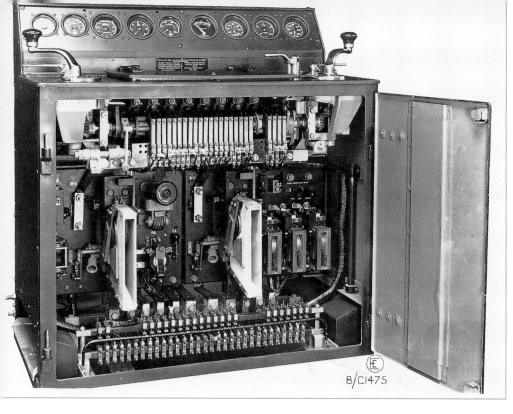

Left: *The underside of the standard 0-6-0 driving desk contains the main control equipment, including the hard linkage between the two master power controllers which operate together. The front of the cabinet was fitted with two hinged removable doors. The main contactors fitted with arc chutes can be seen in the middle.*
Author's collection

Below: *Class 03 cab controls. 1. Master on/off switch, 2. Cab socket fuse, 3. Oil pressure fuse, 4. Front light fuse, 5. Rear light fuse, 6. Heater fuse, 7. Wiper fuse, 8. Oil pressure warning lamp, 9. Ammeter, 10. Water temperature gauge, 11. Oil pressure warning lamp, 12. Front light switches (x 2), 13. Panel light switch, 14. Cab heat switches, 15. Cab light switch, 16. Rear light switches (x2), 17. Gearbox air pressure, 18. Vacuum brake gauge, 19. Duplex pressure gauge, 20. Brake pipe pressure gauge, 21. Lub oil pressure gauge, 22. Rev counter, 23. Speedometer, 24. Fuel gauge, 25. Sanding control valve, 26. Forward/reverse lever, 27. Throttle, 28. Locomotive brake valve, 29. Horn valve, 30. Gear selector, 31. Train brake valve. The cab illustrated is from No 03059. Michael J. Collins*